Sunshine

in my

Pocket

Jennifer French

Outskirts Press, Inc.
Denver, Colorado

"In Memory of My Mother,
Margaret Louise Matlock Thomas"

For My Daughters, Aunts, Grandmothers, Sisters,
Nieces, and all the other remarkable women in my
life...

For my husband, Robert...

And for Jared Knock, who told me at high school
graduation I'd write a book some day..

...And for Daddy...
You're never, ever, alone.

Throughout my life, I have seen many movies about tornadoes. They're all the same: a family runs frantically to an outdoor shelter, one family member (usually the father) barely gets the cellar door shut in time, then the roof comes off the house and a car or two fly into the side of some large building, most commonly a silo or a barn. If the movie's budget was really good, we might also see a flying cow..

Then, all gets calm. A less-seasoned viewer of tornado flicks might think the storm has passed. Those of us that have seen more than one man vs. the elements movie, however, know that they are only in the "eye of the storm." The second wave is coming.

We were our parents' second wave- Hallie, myself, and then Carrie.

The older children were teenagers when Mama found out Hallie was on her way- my mother, in her mid 30s at the time, didn't think she would ever have a child of her own. She had taken on David, the son of her childhood friend, when he was seven. She assumed he'd be the only child she'd ever raise. Then, she met Daddy and became a step-mother and figured that was all the family she'd ever have for herself.

But sometimes life surprises a person.

She said it took seven home pregnancy tests before she was convinced. Then, in August of 1981, Hallie was born.

As shocking as one baby was to her, I don't imagine there's any way she ever expected two more, but she and God both knew that if anyone could handle it, it was she.

"Character is higher than intellect. A great soul will be strong to live as well as think."

–Ralph Waldo Emerson

I met my mother in the wee morning hours of Friday April 6, 1984, and while I certainly don't remember our meeting, I feel like I do. She told me the story many times.

On Thursday, my mother had begun experiencing what she thought might be contractions as she cleaned the house. My older half-brother, Frank, and half-sister, Laura, were at school, but Hallie was only about to turn three in August, so she was at home with Mama. My daddy was a trucker, and was out on the road and Mama, knowing there was nobody else to come get Hallie until the older kids got out of school, managed to avoid going to the doctor all day. She joked later on that she just crossed her legs and hoped I was as slow moving as the others.

When it started getting close to time for the school bus to run, she began cooking supper and when the older ones made it in, she held on long enough for them to do their homework and eat. After dinner, she put together a slop bucket to take out to the hogs, and her water broke while she was carrying the bucket to the barn. It was then that she realized in all her daily activities of cleaning house, cooking dinner, and preparing for my arrival, she had forgotten to pack her hospital bag.

After informing Frank and Laura that I was well on my way, she instructed them to get some clothes ironed. Frank set to work ironing for her, and Laura set to work packing toiletries. My mother, seeing her last opportunity for rest before caring for a newborn, put a towel down in her old wicker rocking chair and watched Wheel of Fortune while she waited for Frank and Laura to finish. When they brought her the bag, it was only about two minutes until the beginning of the Bonus round, so she decided to just finish the show- Hell, I'd held on this long. She was sure I'd hang on a little longer.

Finally Frank, probably afraid he'd have to deliver me himself, told Mama she needed to get in the truck and he'd take her to the hospital.

"Are you crazy?" she asked, before confiscating the keys. She reminded Frank and Laura that they had school in the morning and kissed Hallie good night as she headed out the door. "When Daddy calls, tell him I'm at the hospital," she called back, "Alice will be here later for Hallie."

Then, all alone, she climbed up into her old Ford pick-up and took off into town, stopping halfway at a phone booth to call home and remind my brother and sister not to let our grandmother- Dad's mom- know that she had gone in to have me. She said she didn't need anybody showing up wanting to hold her hand or anything.

When she arrived at the hospital, they put her in a chair in the waiting room while they tried to contact her doctor, who she later found out was somewhere watching "This is Spinal Tap." She waited for him for two hours. When he finally made it in, the nurses began prepping her room. She was still in the waiting room when a lady came in with a young son, about three years of age. He was crying, because he had a very sick stomach. When the nurses came to get Mom, who by this point had been in labor for hours already, she told them to take the little boy first. They wouldn't let her give up her spot, though, so she reluctantly went back with the nurses to the de-livery room, where her doctor was waiting to tell her all about the movie. She labored with me for about eight more hours, and when I was born there we were.

It was just me and her in that room. Daddy was on his way home and the other children were anx-iously awaiting a ride to come meet me.

Legend has it, she told me it was just us, and that I was special to her because we did it ourselves, with nobody else, and I smiled. I don't remember, of course, but I've never doubted her word.

My earliest memory is finding out that my mother was pregnant with her third and final daughter- Carrie. I couldn't have been much more than 2 and a half when they told me the news.

In those days, I was a Golden Girls fanatic. My mother allowed me to watch the show, probably assuming that because it was a show about elderly women it had to be pretty tame. I guess it was a lucky break for her that most of their dialog went so far over my head that I didn't bother trying to figure it out. I liked their house, and I thought they were snazzy dressers for old ladies. I wondered what my mom would dress like when she got old, and how a lady as old as Blanche could possibly still have red hair.

I watched quite a bit of television while my mother was pregnant. It seemed she was always tired. And always sick. She threw up a lot, I remember.

I was eating crackers and Velveeta cheese when Laura, whom I idolized, came to sit next to me on the couch. I casually rested my chin on my hand, which was my trick to looking cool.

"Mama's gonna have a baby girl," Laura said. I was torn between being happy to have her talking to me and wanting her to leave. Rose, my favorite Golden Girl, was talking about a lost lottery ticket and I was trying to keep up with the storyline.

"Uh-huh," I nodded, halfway hoping she'd think I was so cool I couldn't be shocked, and the other hoping she'd go back into the kitchen and leave me with my shows.

"She's going to name her Carrie Marie, like baby Carrie in the Laura Ingalls Wilder books!" Laura explained. I didn't know who Laura Ingalls Wilder was, nor did I care. Dorothy was on the phone with a homeless shelter, tracking down the coat that had the lottery ticket in the pocket. I couldn't turn away from the television now. I had to find out what the lottery was, and if it had a concession stand.

Laura walked back into the kitchen, laughing to her boyfriend, "She doesn't care- I don't think she understands." I was a bit insulted. I did understand, although she was correct in the assumption that I didn't care. I knew what a baby was, and that my mother was going to have one. I got that part. In fact, a baby might be nice- Hallie didn't like the Golden Girls so much and a new TV buddy would be great. I started thinking about all the things I could do with a baby. My dolls heads were always popping off when I tried to change their clothes- maybe a baby would be more resilient. I could certainly practice my clothing methods on the baby before moving on and actually continuing to dress and undress my dolls. It would save everyone a lot of undue frustrations, especially my Daddy and Frank who always had to pop the heads back in.

I heard something at the sliding glass door. It was Red, a neighborhood stray. Red was some sort of Golden Retriever mix, whom at that moment was looking right at me. He would stop by our house once in a while and stay a few days, but never longer than my mother needed him to. He only hung out long enough for her to clean the refrigerator and use him as a garbage disposal. Then, after fertilizing the lawn, he'd disappear again.

He was a drifter, and I'm pretty sure he had several families. Once, he came to visit us and brought about five of his friends. I think that was the only time Mama wasn't happy to see him.

I waited for Golden Girls to end, although he had already distracted me from any explanation of the word "Lottery." I only looked up in time to see the closing credits. M*A*S*H* was on next and I hated that show. Forlorn, I walked to the glass door to look at Red up close.

I always preferred to watch him through the glass- he couldn't knock me over if he couldn't touch me. He sat on the other side and smiled back.

"Mama's having a baby," I told him. I wanted to share the big news for once, instead of always being told. He just stared back at me, blankly.

This is when it first dawned on me that I wasn't going to be the baby anymore. I was just another big kid now, and if Mama had bothered to ask me, I would have told her there were too many big kids in our family as it was. She didn't need another one.

"Do you have a baby sister?" I asked Red. He just stared back at me some more. I bet he did, though. Mama's friend Alice had lots of dogs, so I knew that all dogs had lots of siblings. I'd seen puppies be born before.

"I don't want to be a big kid," I said, shaking my

head at the dog on the other side of the glass, "I won't be a big kid." I thought about Red, and his multiple families. "If I don't like the baby, I'll find a new family and I'll be their baby, okay? Do you know another family that needs a baby?" I waited for him to answer. As a child, and even sometimes now, I have believed that dogs are more wise than people. There's a look they get that lets you know they know. Dogs can predict earthquakes, tsunamis, cancer, seizures, and even death- who's to say they don't know and understand more? Just because they can't say it in words doesn't mean they don't know.

So on that day to anyone else, Red was just panting and wagging his tail- the typical dog response to anything any person tells them. But I was just a child, so I saw the wink. Everything and everybody winks for the same reason, even God. My Grandmother Hallie, Mom's mother, used to say that God sends winks when we need them. When you're having a bad day, and a child smiles at you in the grocery store, or you find lost money in your pants pockets, or your favorite movie comes on TV- That's a God wink.

I looked at Red, and knew what his wink meant.
"It'll be okay, kid," he grinned.

I don't know how much time passed between that day and Carrie's arrival. It seems like it was the very same day, but in my heart I know that's not the case. I don't remember where Hallie and I were while

Mama had Carrie, but I remember the hospital and going to meet her for the first time.

She was bigger than I thought she'd be. She had a very round, purple face and white hair that stuck straight up from the top of her misshapen head. Daddy called her "Fuzzy."

She started crying, and it was such an obnoxious screeching sound that I was certain my parents wouldn't keep her very long. They'd be tired of her within a week, and I'd be the baby again. I just had to wait them out. Once, my mother got a coffee pot for Christmas, but she returned it to the store and instead got a beautiful blanket for her bed. I wondered what we could get for a baby.

When I crawled up onto the bed next to my mother and looked at my little sister, though, I changed my mind.

Fuzzy was beautiful up close. She was prettier than any baby doll I'd ever seen, and was certainly cuter than that baby in all those stupid toilet paper commercials. I started hoping the screeching would work itself out quickly. I didn't want them to trade Fuzzy for a toaster.

The next day, when Fuzzy came home, I considered her my baby. I did everything I possibly could to assist Mama in her mothering - and Mama graciously accepted my help. I was given such tasks as finding the baby wipes, carrying dirty diapers to the garbage, standing on a chair and holding onto the towel while Mama bathed Fuzzy in the sink, and- the most important of all jobs- lying down on Mama's bed and taking a nap with Fuzzy so she wouldn't be afraid. I even learned to love the screeching. In fact, the only thing that bothered me about Fuzzy in those first couple of weeks was a black plug of some sort sticking out of her belly button. Mama explained, the best she could I imagine, that it was her umbilical stump and that the black plug was a special bandage. I completely misunderstood, though, and thought that Fuzzy ate through a hole in her stomach and the plug was to hold the food in. I decided I didn't like it - it was big and dark and painful looking. I wanted Fuzzy to have a happy belly- not one with some ugly ornament attached. Every day, I asked Mama when we could unplug Fuzzy. Every day, Mama said maybe tomorrow. Then, the glorious day came.

"Jenny!" Mama screamed from the bedroom, "It's time!"

My little heart pounded as I ran down the hall and climbed up onto Mama's bed. The little black plug was barely hanging on Fuzzy's belly. All it was going to take was one little pluck, and Fuzzy's navel would be liberated.

"Don't hurt her," Mama said, "But go ahead and pull it off."

The whole thing, in hindsight, is pretty sick. But nervousness and a sense of importance swelled up in me. I had to do a wonderful job of this- I couldn't let Mama or Fuzzy down. As I put my little fingers on the end of the plug, I had visions of Fuzzy deflating and flying around the room like a balloon that had come untied. That awful blowing sound filled my head. Oh no.. What if Fuzzy flew out the window and got stuck in a tree?

I turned to make sure the windows were shut. "Go on," Mama urged, "Or would you rather I do it?"

"No, I can do it!" I yelled back, and with that- I plucked. Fuzzy barely flinched, and there I was with the plug in my hand. The whole thing was very anti-climatic. I don't know what I thought would happen- other than Fuzzy deflating and flying out the window. Maybe that's what I was hoping for. It would certainly have been more exciting.

This, however, was my first lesson in disappointment.

Fuzzy grew quite large in a very short amount of time, and soon her personality started shining through.

Fuzzy wasn't quite the television buddy I had hoped for. She was actually quite worrisome, with her constant prowling. I just knew she was going to get into trouble if she wasn't careful. Fuzzy was a late walker, so she crawled throughout the house, searching for things to get into.

She had mammoth feet that she drug behind her when she crawled. Once, I watched her crawl across the pink carpeting in my mother's bedroom. Her giant feet left tracks behind her, and I had to show somebody. I called Mama into the bedroom and showed her and, not surprisingly, she was as amazed as I. In fact, she went to the bedroom door and yelled "John! Get in here! It looks like someone drove a 4-wheeler through the bedroom!"

Fuzzy just looked over her shoulder and asked, "What?"

"What" was Fuzzy's first word, and she used it frequently.

Fuzzy's large feet led to another problem for my mother- it was impossible to find shoes that fit. Fuzzy's feet were not only large, but they were as wide as they were long. My father once suggested we tape butter bowls around them. Mama laughed his suggestion off as a joke, but I only really think he was about forty percent kidding.

My mother was able to find one particular brand of shoes that fit Fuzzy properly, but was afraid to buy more than one pair at a time because of Fuzzy's feet growing at breakneck speed. Because Fuzzy didn't much care for shoes, she would throw one or both out the window at every opportunity. This left Fuzzy barefoot about half the time.

As time wore on, Mama made us start calling Fuzzy by her proper name, out of fear it would stick and she would wind up with a very large-footed thirty year old daughter named Fuzz.

When Laura and Frank left home for good, Mama and Daddy decided to hunt a house in the country, I guess to give Carrie's feet more room to expand and so we could have cows.

While decorating, Mama hung a map of the United States on a bulletin board in the kitchen and put a thumbtack over where our house was. Every night from then on, when Daddy was on the road and would call home, she'd move the tack to wherever he was. We would watch as the tack got further from home, then closer again. We were amazed at how far our father traveled. Once, he went all the way into Alaska.

While Daddy was gone, Mama kept us busy with trips to the creek. There was a creek within walking distance of the house, and she'd put on her bathing suit, and strip Hallie, Carrie, and myself down to our underwear and we'd go swimming. I'd try to catch minnows in a jar while Hallie tried to learn how to swim. Carrie just hung her feet into the water, afraid to get in. Mama would sit in the water and cool off and play with us.

These were good days, easy days.

I remember how beautiful my mother would look down at the creek. Her skin was as brown as the water, and her blonde hair reflected the sunlight. She glowed. It's hard to believe, looking back, that she was already sick.

"We need cancer because, by the very fact of it's insurability, it makes all other diseases, however virulent, not cancer."

–Gilbert Adair

The first time I heard the "c" word, I was five. The doctor had told Mama while she was pregnant with Carrie that something "wasn't right," but she ignored him. She figured any abnormalities in her screenings were from being 40 and pregnant. After Carrie was born, she felt alright and didn't give the doctor's concerns another thought until the bleeding.

She thought it was just another period, but five days turned to ten, then ten days turned to twenty and it didn't stop. We didn't know all this at the time, we just knew Mama wasn't feeling well. She left us with Laura when she went to the doctor. Then back again. Then again. And one more time.

I don't remember the day we found out. I don't remember who told us. I just remember the feeling in our house changed. Before she got sick, she would hug us like mothers do. Daddy would laugh and play with us like Daddies do. Mama and Daddy would look at and hug each other like any other married couple. But, after Mama got sick, the hugs changed. The looks changed. Every time Daddy played with us, I could sense that he was more worried about the distraction than the fun. Mama's hugs always felt like she thought they were her last. Daddy looked at Mama with apologies in his eyes. He was sorry, for what- we didn't know. She looked at him the same way- She was sorry, too, for some reason. Now that I'm older, I know he was sorry he couldn't help her, and she was sorry that he might be left to raise us alone. Their hugs even stopped looking like hugs. They were holding on for dear life, like if they let go of each other, they each might fall off opposite ends of the earth.

We knew Mama was very sick, and that she needed us to be good and that we were brave little girls because everyone told us so. And we also knew that Mama was strong, and that Daddy loved her and us more than anything in the whole world and that everyone promised the three of us girls would always be together. No matter what.

I think it was my Uncle Clyde that I first heard say the "c" word out loud. We were sitting in the living room, watching Indiana Jones on his big screen like we did every time we went to his house. He and Daddy and Mama and Aunt Evonne were in the kitchen, and I heard him say it. I didn't know what cancer was, but I knew it was bad. People on television were always afraid of getting it.

I looked at Hallie, and she nodded at me. She had already figured out what was wrong with Mama, but I was younger and slower than she was. I remember neither of us said a word to each other, but when we heard the word we laid down next to each other on that huge couch and she put her arms around me and we laid there, in complete silence, for the next couple of hours until it was time to go home.

I didn't know about death. I wasn't afraid of that. I'm not sure what I was afraid of. Just Mama being sick, I suppose. I was afraid because everyone else was afraid. That night, when I hugged Mama good night, I asked her if she was feeling better. She nodded, and said she felt great. I looked into her big, gorgeous blue eyes and just knew it was the truth. It had to be.

Mama wouldn't lie.

Daddy couldn't quit his job. We needed the money too bad. My parents weren't wealthy.

Several neighbors and friends of Mama and Daddy's came together to help us while Mama was sick. Mama had to travel from our home in Waverly, Tennessee to Nashville frequently for her radiation treatments. Chemotherapy wasn't an option for her because the type of cancer she had would not have responded to it.

At the time, we just had a pick up, and it had no

air conditioning and the power steering wasn't that great. This was before the days of car seat enforcement, so Mama would put all three of us in the truck with her- Laura or Alice, my Mama's best friend, would accompany us on the trips. Whichever one of them came would have Carrie on their lap the entire time. Hallie would sit next to them, and I'd sit next to Mama, who always insisted on driving to her appointments unless she was feeling too weak. The drive was a little over an hour, and we'd be hot and exhausted by the time we made it to the hospital, then it would be a couple hours in the waiting room before we could head home.

When Mama would go in for an MRI, the nurses would sneak us back to radiology with them. We'd sit in the glass room, and talk to Mama through the speakers. She couldn't talk back because they needed her to sit perfectly still, but she'd smile and give us a little wave as the table she laid on moved into the MRI machine. It looked like such a scary machine to me. I would always tell her not to be scared, and the nurses would laugh. I thought that was incredibly rude of them- to laugh at my Mama, who was so obviously afraid. She was crying, after all.

On days she got treatments, she was always weak when we'd leave the hospital. Alice or Laura would drive home, and she'd hold Carrie in the passenger seat. Once, we blew a tire on the way back to Waverly. Laura was with us, but she, herself was pregnant. She pulled the truck over to the side of the road, and she and Mama got out together to change it.

I remember watching Laura start to pick the tire up to put it in the back of the truck, and Mama stopping her. "You don't need to be lifting that," Mama said. Then, she put her whole body into lifting that tire, and couldn't do it. Instead, she fell forward onto it.

"Margaret," Laura said, "Let me.."

Cars whizzed by, but none of them bothered stopping. Even as a child, barely even school age, I could see grown men driving by this pregnant girl and this sick woman trying to change a tire and not stopping and I wondered what was wrong with them. Were they blind? My daddy would have stopped. So would my big brother.

Mama shook her head, stood up, and tried again. This time she did it, but it took everything she had. They both got back in the truck crying.

"Are you okay?" Laura asked. Mama struggled to catch her breath.

"I'm fine," she said, "Just get me home."

When we'd get home, Mama would take Hallie, Carrie, and I to her bedroom and get out the Jergen's lotion. She'd lay on her bed, and ask us to rub lotion on her arms and legs. We would, and she'd make a big fuss out of how good it felt, and how good we were at what we did. But we all knew better.

She didn't do it because her legs were dry, or because it felt good.

She did it to keep us in that room with her, because she didn't have the energy to keep up with us if she let us roam further than her bedroom door. The lotion trick was her insurance that we were safe, because as long as we were on that bed with her, nothing could happen to us. And, maybe, she felt that nothing could happen to her, either.

I loved rubbing lotion on her legs, though, whatever the reason. When we were done, she'd have us lay down next to her in that big bed, and she'd tell us how much she loved us. And we'd fall asleep there, with the sun shining in the window on that yellow comforter. A mother and three little girls, sleeping soundly, bathed in golden sunlight.. the vision of happiness, and health, and safety..

And above all else, love..

Soon, the children, the cancer, and the house became too much for Mama to deal with alone. I don't know how long we were there, but us three little girls were taken to my Grandma Hallie's house in Chattanooga. It seemed like we were there for a very long time, but I don't think it was.

Grandma Hallie was a sweet lady. She lived in an old house with an old barn. She rented stables out to people that wanted the convenience of living in the city, but the novelty of owning a horse. I loved her house. It was always very clean, and smelled like her perfume. Except her pantry. Her pantry smelled like bananas and coffee grounds- the most beautiful smell in the world. Even now, I'll catch that perfect combination of smells in the grocery store, and linger for just a minute, taking it in.

Grandma's yard smelled like horses, and sometimes we would walk to the fence with sugar cubes or apples for them, and we all had our favorites. Mine was Reno. He was big and white with gray spots. I always thought he looked very old and wise, like my grandmother. I told Grandma one day that I wished he was my horse, though, and I'd name him Dimes for her, because his gray spots looked like dimes.

My Grandma Hallie loved dimes. She loved how they shined. She loved the size of them, the feel of them- she once said that all anyone would ever have to do to make her happy in her old age was to give her a bowl of dimes to run her fingers in. She loved how tiny and smooth they were.

Most of all, though, she said she loved how- even though they were the smallest coin- they were worth more than a penny or nickel. They could do more and go farther than these two other coins that were much larger. Kind of poetic, when you think about it..

For the first day or so, I think we were all pretty excited about being at Grandma's house, but soon we got homesick. We all missed Mama terribly. I remember waking up every morning I was there and, having no sense of time, wondering if this was the day Daddy promised to come back to get us.

But Grandma was wonderful. She spoiled us. Our Aunts, Sheila & Carol, and our cousin, Ashley, came to see us nearly every day we were there. They all spoiled us. But I just wanted my mother.

One day, I was playing in the back room of my Grandmother's house, the yellow room is what we called it. I heard Grandma in the "dark room," which was actually just another bedroom where she stored some things she wasn't using. The dark room always gave me the creeps. That's where my sisters, my cousins, and I would go to tell ghost stories when we were kids. In my memory, it's a huge room- it couldn't have been very big. Grandma's house wasn't very big.

If I remember correctly, the walls were painted dark green. I think there was some old brown carpeting on the floor. Boxes were stacked up against the walls, and on the wall hung "the picture." Grandma had a photograph taken of her sister, who had died as a child. Hattie, Grandma's sister, was only about two or three in the photograph and it was an old photograph- from back when they blurred if the subject didn't sit still. It always looked like a photograph of a ghost to us. We were afraid of that picture, and as silly as it is now, I remember my sister and I daring each other to sit in the dark room with Hattie for four minutes. I don't know why it was always four minutes, and not five or three. It made sense to us at the time, though.

When I heard Grandma in the dark room that day, I was worried. I didn't want her to be locked in there alone with Hattie, so I decided to look in on her. I hated the dark room. When I walked in, the picture of Hattie stared down at me, and I thought about running back out into the yellow room where I would be safe. I was drawn in, though, by what my grandmother was doing.

She had a box open, and was pulling out strips of fabric. It was the most beautiful fabric I had ever seen- yellow and red and green, with little flowers on it. Some of it was striped and other strips were just solid colors. I couldn't wait to see what she was going to do with it all.

"Grandma, what is that for?" I asked her, my attention now turned to her sewing box- and a little red pin cushion. It looked like a tomato. I wanted it.

"You and your sister and me are going to do something special for your Mama," she explained. I could hardly wait. I wanted so badly to do something to impress my mommy. Maybe if I put the effort in to make it extra special, she wouldn't have to leave me behind anymore.

Over the next few days, we helped Grandma sew the patches together. Grandma hand-sewed every-thing, and taught us to do so as well. Of course, our stitches weren't anywhere near as tight or perfectly straight as the ones Grandma did, but that's what made it special.

Before long, the strips of fabric had been patched together to form a gorgeous quilt. I couldn't wait to see my mother's face when she got it. But I don't remember that part.

I'm not sure when Mom got the quilt. If she got it when we were picked up or if Grandma mailed it to her. I'm not even entirely sure the quilt was totally done when we got picked up. I just know she got it and I grew up seeing it, and that she said the most wonderful part was the patches that were falling apart, because they were done by Hallie and me, with our little kid hands, and our imperfect sewing. The imperfections were her proof that the quilt had been a joint effort, and every loose stitch was done with love.

The day finally came when Daddy picked us up. I remember being so excited to see Mama again. And I remember the whole long car ride back to Waverly from Chattanooga, sleeping with my head against Daddy's arm, smelling Marlboro's and Stetson, and knowing that things would be better soon. Daddy was here.

It's funny that I remember the tomato pin cush-ion, and Reno, and how Grandma's pantry smelled because I don't remember when Mama got the "all clear" from the doctor.

But I do remember the county fair.

Everyone we saw wanted to hug Mama, and tell her how happy they were for her, and how- for a while there- they'd been scared. Everyone was so happy. There was a big ride that turned upside down and tossed cars around. It had a picture of Batman on it, and people screamed inside. Someone told my mother that their cousin had ridden it three times, and thrown up every turn. She wanted to ride it, and Aunt Evonne volunteered to get on with her if she was sure she was up for it. "I beat Cancer," Mama joked,

"I can handle this."

I stayed on the ground with Laura and watched the ride toss my mother around. She'd wave every time her car rolled by. Once, she blew a kiss. She wasn't scared at all, and I was so proud of her. I told an old man that was my mom up there, and he just laughed. Nobody understood how brave she was. Not like I did.

After she got off the Batman ride, she scooped me up in her arms. Carrie was with Alice and Hallie had run off with Daddy. "I want to ride something," I told her. She carried me on her hip all over the fair until we found the Scrambler. She asked if I wanted to ride it with her and I said I did, but really I was a little scared. She and I rode it four times together. She smiled and laughed the whole time. I was afraid, but I couldn't let her know that. She was my big brave Mama. I had to be big and brave, too. When I felt like screaming, I'd bury my face in her arm, and smell her clothes. After the fourth time, Daddy, Hallie, Alice, Laura, and Carrie were waiting. It was time for us all to go home. Mama picked me up and carried me to the car, and never stopped laughing. She was truly happy that day. Relieved.

Free.

"There are nights when the wolves are silent, and only the moon howls."

–George Carlin

W hen I was a little girl, Mama's friend, Alice, was my best friend, too.

Alice, actually, was once my mother's aunt. She had been married to Mom's uncle, then Mom's uncle died & she remarried Gabe. They lived close to us when Mama and Daddy lived on Turkey Creek and Alice would baby-sit me and my sisters when Mama needed to run an errand or have a few minutes alone.

She was an older lady. She was short and had dark hair and smiling eyes. Her face was wrinkled, but not the kind of wrinkling that you imagine comes from a hard life or sadness. Her wrinkles were more or less proof that she knew how to laugh.

She had the coolest stuff. She had a clock that was shaped like a cat. Its eyes darted back and forth and its tail wagged to count the seconds. I coveted that clock. I wished so many times that she would give it to me.

Along with the clock, she had the largest VHS collection I had ever seen, with movies that ranged from "Gone with the Wind" to "Major Payne." "Major Payne" was her favorite movie. That seems so funny now.

Gabe raised hunting dogs- mostly Beagles, but he had a few coon hounds thrown in. Alice also had a couple Basset Hounds that she would sometimes breed.

And a poodle named Blondie.

Alice was a rescuer as well. There was, at one point, a baby skunk in a cage in her bedroom and a chipmunk in a cardboard box in the kitchen. I loved that chipmunk. I named him Alvin and when he died, Alice and I cried together.

I loved Alice. I loved the way it felt when she'd hug me. I loved how her house always smelled like she'd just cooked breakfast. I loved to sit in the little restaurant booth she had in her kitchen and she'd talk to me like I was a grown up. We'd talk about important things, like Gremlins and barn owls and puppies and why shoes leave black marks on tile floors. Things that were so important, I just knew nobody but her would ever understand.

Once, Alice gave me one of her puppies. She let me pick him out all on my own. He was half basset hound, and half beagle. I named him Rocky, and he was short and fat and, when he ran, his ears drug on the ground. I loved Rocky to pieces.

While Hallie was at school, Alice and Mama

would bring Carrie and I with them to pick black-berries, and I'd always ask to bring Rocky with me. Alice would let him ride in her car, and Carrie and I would play with Rocky while Alice and Mama filled their empty milk jugs. They always talked about making blackberry jelly, but I don't remember them ever doing it. I guess they must have.

Sometimes, Gabe would tell us about the Bell Witch. In actuality, the real story of the Bell Witch takes place in Adams, Tennessee, which is well over an hour out of Waverly. We were convinced, though, that she would make a special trip to Waverly just to eat us. And Gabe only reinforced that notion in our little heads. A couple times, we would be at Alice and Gabe's after dark, and Daddy and Gabe would sit together on the front porch swing, drinking beer, cackling and howling just to scare us. We knew it was just Daddy and Gabe, but it was more fun to believe the witch had made her trip. We'd scream and hide in Alice's living room, and she would go out on the porch and scold the two of them for being so mean to us.

I absolutely adored Alice. When I started Kin-dergarten, I talked about Alice to my classmates all the time. I was lucky to have a grown up friend- they just had their Mommies and Daddies. I had better.

One day, she came to my kindergarten class. My teacher must have already been notified that Alice was picking me up early, because she didn't ask any questions. She just let me go.

I'm not sure why Alice picked me up early that

day- my mother must have told her to, but she didn't pick up Hallie and Carrie was not with her. I have always enjoyed telling myself that Alice asked specifically for me and begged for the privilege of picking me up and having me all to herself. I'm sure this wasn't the case, but I'll believe whatever I want.

That was a fun day. She and I went and got ice cream cones. They weren't like the ice cream cones my mother bought at the store though. They were actually pointed cones and the lady at the ice cream shop put two scoops on it- and the two scoops were different colors. They were like the ice cream cones you see on cartoons. I thought I must have been super important to get a cartoon ice cream cone.

Then, Alice took me to the grocery store where they were having some sort of street fair. There were clowns in the parking lot, showing children magic tricks. One of them pulled a plastic checkerboard ring out of my ear. I didn't know how he managed it, but I was impressed. He then got down on one knee and proposed marriage. That part was a little embarrassing, but I graciously accepted his proposal and he told me he'd call me. He never did. That bastard.

We went to the pet store. Her poodle needed something. I can't remember what it was, though, and there were kittens in the pet store and I wanted one so badly, but my mother would never let me have a kitten that had to live inside. I knew this. My mother hated cats. Alice told me she'd work on it for me.

When we got back to Alice's house, I scooted up into that restaurant booth and she was unloading her groceries. She handed me a Little Debbie brownie. I didn't even have to ask for one- she knew I'd want it. Alice and I had that kind of connection. Eating the brownie, I got to thinking about my big sister.

Hallie was a girl scout. Her troop was the brownie troop.

I didn't understand girl scouts. My mother had taken me along with her to one of my sister's troop meetings once, and I was quite frankly a little scared of it. There was some secret society of big kids and they were all dressed alike and wore stupid sashes and recited a poem or something. When they recited their poem in unison, it sounded an awful lot like chanting, and I'd seen things on television about secret societies that chant. I wanted no part in it.

The night of that troop meeting, I was riding in my mother's car looking at the moon. I wondered how it could always be wherever I was, but other people always had it where they were, too. Was there more than one moon? Did it just follow around the people who are looking at it?

I decided I needed to ask Alice.

"Alice," I asked, "Why does the moon always follow me?"

Alice chuckled. I swung my feet under the table, waiting for her reply.

"It doesn't follow you, Jenny," She said, "It's just so big, and so high up that everyone can see it."

Her explanation didn't make much sense to me,

but I accepted it. If it came from Alice, it must be true.

Alice thought for a minute, quietly, and smiled, "Jenny, I want to make a secret deal with you."

I was excited. I loved having secrets with Alice and couldn't wait to hear what she had to tell me. I looked up at her & smiled, nodding my agreement.

"No matter what happens or wherever you go or I go or how far apart we are, before you go to bed every night, look at the moon for me. Look out your window or go outside- whatever you have to do. And when you see the moon, I want you to think about your day and think of me and I'll do the same for you. And we'll always do that together. Every night. And we won't be doing it alone because we both know the other is somewhere doing the same."

This sounded like a lot of fun to me because I was a little girl and it was a secret. I promised Alice I would. I guarded this secret with my life. I was well into adulthood before I told anyone of mine and Alice's secret deal.

"Your current safe boundaries were once unknown frontiers."

–Author Unknown

W e didn't know what Mama was thinking as she loaded our suitcases into that old New Yorker.

"Let's go see Aunt Camille," Mama said, as if her sister only lived a mile or two down the road. I didn't remember Aunt Camille, but Mama said I had a cousin my age named Timmy, so I was ready to go. It would be nice to play with a cousin.

Hallie was crying as we got in the car. Mama put her in the front seat, Carrie and I took the back.

"Why is Hallie crying?" I asked.

"She thinks Daddy's going to be mad at us," Mama said, "But he won't. I promise."

"We're never coming back," Hallie said.

Mama quickly interrupted, and "Yes we are. This is just a visit." I felt better that Mama said so, but I still worried. Why would Hallie say such a thing, unless she already knew? I always trusted Hallie's judgment, for she was nearly three years older and wiser than I.

"What is South Dakota?" I asked. I had never heard of such a place in all my six years.

"It's the place with the mountain that has all the people's heads carved in it," Hallie answered.

This was the source of much confusion for several miles, wondering which head Aunt Camille lived in. Eventually, though, I gave up worrying about it. I figured I'd see when I got there.

"It's a long car ride," Mama warned, "So y'all just go to sleep if you get tired. You have your pillows, don't you?"

We nodded and settled in. We were used to long car rides. It couldn't be that bad. We'd been to Nashville and Chattanooga. How far away could South Dakota be?

We drove for hours before Mama stopped for lunch. We stopped at McDonald's, but it wasn't any McDonald's I recognized. It wasn't Waverly. I was getting worried.

"We should just go home," I told Mama, "Maybe Aunt Camille wants to come see us."

"Aunt Camille is expecting us at her house," Mama answered, "And we've come too far to turn back now."

"What if Daddy comes home," I asked, "And he has no supper?"

"I left him a note," she answered, "He'll know where to find us."

Wait, I thought, *a note? She's driving us halfway to Jupiter and she left him a note?*

Oh man, he was going to be mad... Hallie was right..

I ate my happy meal in the backseat, and looked at the upholstery on the car door. Mama had bought the New Yorker from Uncle Clyde and Aunt Evonne just a few months before. They had no children and it was as neat as the day they bought it when they handed the keys over. It was the nicest car Mama had ever owned, and now there were holes in the doors. Carrie and I had invented a game of biting through the upholstery. I don't know why we thought we needed to do such a thing, but it was a lot of fun for us. It made us feel powerful. We'd bite big chunks out of the faux leather, leaving the white cushioning sticking out everywhere. Then we'd just laugh while Mama yelled, "Why'd you do that? Are you goats? God Bless America!"

Mama had a habit of inventing cuss words that weren't really cuss words. She had terrible road rage, and, either at us or other motorists, would cut loose with a string of almost-expletives that would have us rolling for hours. Sometimes, she'd slip up and a few real cuss words would work their way in, like the time she got lost then had someone cut in front of her while she was looking for Aunt Carol's apartment. She laid on her horn and yelled "Look at that pig assed doorknob pissing crock shit!" Mama was my hero.

When she wasn't complaining, her car was.

When she'd start the old New Yorker, it would always say "Please fasten your seatbelts." When something went wrong under the hood, it would say "Please Service Soon."

Our favorite, though, was when a door wouldn't be quite closed all the way, and it would say "A door is ajar." Sometimes, we'd purposely leave our doors open a little bit, just so it would remind us. Then, we'd laugh and yell back, "Is it a jelly jar?"

That's insanely funny when you're six.

We rode for hours more before Mama found her way to a hotel and we checked in for the night. I'd never stayed in a hotel before. I was impressed that such places existed. I wondered how many hotels my daddy had slept in, since he spent so many nights away from home.

Mama ordered pizza, and they delivered it to us. I thought they only did that in movies. I couldn't believe it was a real service they offered. Mama gave him twenty dollars, and told him to keep the change. I knew then what I wanted to be when I grew up. Twenty dollars was a lot of money.

Our room just had one king-sized bed in it, and the four of us slept together in that bed that night. It was the biggest bed I'd ever seen. Mama told us all how nice Aunt Camille was, and how sweet Uncle Tim would be, and how much we'd get along with Timmy and our other cousin, Catherine, who was Hallie's age.

I missed Rocky. Rocky was at Alice's. "Does Timmy have a dog?" I asked.

"I think so," Mama said, "I'm not sure."

I knew Timmy's dog wouldn't be like Rocky, though. I wondered if I'd ever see Rocky again.

"Will Daddy bring Rocky with him when he comes?" I asked.

"I don't know," she said, "We'll see."

I knew what "we'll see" meant. It was a no. I wished I had hugged him one more time as I drifted off to sleep.

I woke up the next morning with "we'll see" still on my mind. It had occurred to me in my sleep the night before that maybe the "we'll see" wasn't because she knew Daddy wouldn't bring Rocky, but that maybe Daddy wasn't coming. My little heart started panicking. "Daddy's coming, right?" I asked.

"Oh yea," Mama said, "Daddy's coming. It'll be okay."

"You don't know that," Hallie said. Hallie was nine, and far smarter than me. She knew things I couldn't wrap my little head around. Once, Hallie told me that if my second toe was longer than my big toe, it meant I was going to die when I was seven. I believed that until I turned eight. Another time, she told me the reason I had hazel eyes and she and Carrie had blue eyes was because I was adopted. I didn't quite believe her, because Daddy's eyes are hazel, but I always wondered, just a little bit.

"Hallie, I do know he's coming!" Mama snapped back, "Daddy wouldn't just forget about us."

Mama was right. He wouldn't. I rested a little easier knowing Daddy would at least come looking for us. I'd see him again, even if he wasn't bringing Rocky to me.

We made it into Huron, South Dakota in the early afternoon. We came into town on Highway 14. I saw an overpass as we neared town and thought this must be a huge city. I never saw an overpass in Waverly. I desperately wanted Mama to take the exit and cross over the road. I couldn't remember ever riding over one before, but we didn't. Instead, we drove by a hotel and bowling alley with a huge pheasant on top of the building, and a car lot with a big white buffalo. This was a fun place to live, I guessed. They certainly liked animals. Like me and Alice.

We pulled up in front of Aunt Camille's house and she ran out the front door to hug Mama. Catherine and Timmy stood in the doorway, looking out at us.

They didn't look like I expected them to. I don't know what I thought they'd look like, but it wasn't this. Catherine was pretty. I thought she was the prettiest little girl I'd ever met. She had sandy brown hair, cut at her shoulders. Aunt Camille's hair was black, but cut just like Catherine's, and they both wore headbands. Catherine had big, brown eyes and when she smiled her eyes shined. She ran out into the yard and hugged Hallie and they acted like they remembered each other, but I didn't remember Catherine or Timmy or Aunt Camille, and I was fairly certain I'd never been to this house before.

Timmy looked like my cousin Ashley. They both had black hair and freckles. They were also both about my age. I wondered why I didn't have black hair and freckles, since my cousins that were my age both did. I thought about Hallie telling me I was adopted, and was more worried than ever. But this wasn't the time to ask. I heard a dog barking.

"I hear a puppy!" I yelled.

"That's Chris!" Aunt Camille said, "Jenny you've grown so much!"

I wasn't worried about how much I'd grown. I just wanted to see the dog. "Uh huh," I said, "Where's Chris?"

Aunt Camille looked at Timmy, who hadn't yet said anything. "Take her inside and show her Chris. She likes dogs."

Timmy still didn't say anything as he motioned for me to follow him inside. They had Chris in the basement. Their basement was nice- like a second house. I had never seen a basement so nice. There was a living room down there, and a bedroom. And the bedroom had a sink in it. Talk about luxury.

As interesting as their basement was, though, Chris was also worthy of further investigation. He was unlike any dog I'd ever seen. He was a little larger than Alice's beagles, but not much. And his fur wasn't brown and white or even black and white as I'd assumed it would be. He was a silver color. His ears didn't droop like a dog's should, but instead they pointed up. And he had a beard, like a human.

"What kind of dog is he?" I asked. I knew there

were different kinds. Alice had beagles and basset hounds, and Daddy's friend Joe Berry even had a Blue Heeler. And Mama's friend Lorraine had a little dog that looked like a polish sausage. I knew this must just be a different breed than I'd seen before. There had to be a logical explanation.

"He's a schnauzer," Timmy said. I thought this was a funny name for a dog breed, but I didn't question Timmy. He would know better than I would. I just wondered why whoever it is that names dog breeds would stick a name like "Schnauzer" on this dog and call the dog that looked like a sausage something else.

"He's cute," I said.

"Yea," Timmy answered. We stood in silence for a few minutes.

"Do you want to see something?" Timmy asked.

I nodded, and he ran back up the basement stairs. I followed him into his bedroom where pulled several stuffed animals out of a small cupboard above his closet and sat them around his room in various places. Then, he reached under his bed and pulled out a Nerf gun. I couldn't believe he owned one. I'd seen them on television many times, but never thought anyone actually bought them. My mom always told me I couldn't have one. Aunt Camille must have been the most understanding mom in the universe.

Timmy pointed around the room at the stuffed dogs he had sat up. "I used to sleep with them when I was little," he said, one eye squinted as he steadied his arm and aimed, "But now I'm bigger and I don't have to. So I shoot them."

He unloaded his Nerf gun, never missing any of his targets. I was very much impressed, and no longer missed home or Rocky.

Timmy was a cool kid. And this was going to work out just fine.

"If they can make penicillin out of moldy bread, they can sure make something out of you."

–Muhammad Ali

We weren't in Huron long before Daddy joined us, just like Mama said he would.

We were at Aunt Camille's when Mama told us he was on his way and that we were going to get a new house in Huron and live nearby our cousins forever. I was so happy to hear that there was finally going to be someone close by to play with, that it didn't even bother me that we had to leave Rocky behind. He was with Alice, anyway, and I knew she'd take good care of him. Timmy and I had a lot of things we needed to shoot.

When Daddy showed up, we had all kinds of things to tell him about- our trip, for one, and our "new" cousins. Daddy seemed very interested in everything we had to tell him. Carrie, being the baby, was confused as to why Daddy hadn't ridden to South Dakota with us. "Why didn't you come in

Mama's car?" she asked. Hallie and I had wondered, as well, but knew that it was most likely confusing grown up stuff that we wouldn't understand, so hadn't bothered asking.

But Daddy was wise. "I had to stay with Gabe and fight the Bell Witch," he proclaimed, "But don't worry. We got her."

Daddy's always been one to tell crazy stories. He's the king of exaggeration and he's got stories that we've heard a million times in our lives, but we always want to hear them again. As he tells them, the three of us will look at each other- not saying a word, just occasionally giggling because we know what's changed since the last time he's told the story. Snakes, dogs, and angry drunks always grow. Childhood friends get smaller. And he's always thirty years old.

1972 was, evidently, a very busy year for my father.

Mama and Daddy found a house not very far from Aunt Camille. It wasn't a large home. It had one room downstairs, and two upstairs, a small living room, a dining room, a kitchen, and a bathroom. But I thought it was very impressive. It had an upstairs- I couldn't remember ever living where there was an upstairs before. Carrie and I shared the biggest up-stairs bedroom, and Hallie got her own room, which would prove to be the pattern in every house we lived in for the next six or seven years.

Carrie wasn't a bad roommate, really, but I don't think she slept a wink until she was about nine years old and she's still catching up.

At the time, Carrie and I had separate twin beds that sat on opposite sides of the window in our room. I was a little bit afraid of the window. I'd snuck into the living room once and hid behind my Daddy's old chair to watch "Salem's Lot." When I'd go upstairs to that room to sleep at night, I would always turn my face away from the window and promise myself that I wouldn't roll over, no matter what I heard. I just knew that if I did there would be a boy with yellow eyes smiling in at me, and then it would be all over. He'd hypnotize me into inviting him in and bite Carrie and me- then what would we do?

So I would lie there in the darkness, facing the wall, pulling my blankets up to cover my neck, just in case Carrie invited him in. Then, just as I'd be about to fall asleep, the nightly ritual would begin.

"Jenny?" She'd whisper.

"What?" I'd ask, even though I already knew what she wanted.

"Tell me a Legend."

It was hard thinking up legends for her. The whole legend craze started when I was about four and Mama told me about how, one morning, it was so cold that the sky froze and the sun was stuck just over the horizon. Davy Crockett was on his way home from hunting all night when he saw the sun stuck in the sky and he knew that nothing would ever thaw out if the sun didn't rise to warm everything up, so he climbed up the sunrays and took the bear he was carrying on his back and started beating at the ice until it busted apart. Then, he kicked the sun real hard and it rose up quick and thawed the whole world out. He knew nobody would ever believe him, though, so he broke off a piece of the sun to carry around in his pocket before he jumped off and went home. I often wished I had a piece of sunshine in my pocket to carry, but on nights like tonight, a book of Tall Tales would probably be far more beneficial. Eventually, though, I always thought of something.

"Chickens used to be bald," I would have said.

"Then how come they have feathers now?" she would have asked.

"Because all the baby chickens in the world got together one day and decided to eat all the queen bee's honey, but they don't have hands so their wings got all sticky. On the way home, they got lost and hitched a ride on a truck that was delivering pillows, and the feathers from the pillows got stuck to the honey."

She would be satisfied for a while. Then, I'd start drifting off to sleep again, when..

"Where did the feathers in the pillows come from?"

"Geese! Go to sleep!"

"I can't."

"Why can't you go to sleep?" I'd snap, even though this was my favorite part of the nightly ordeal because her excuses were always so lame. Once, she said she couldn't go to sleep because she had a big booger in her nose that wouldn't come out and if she fell asleep it would blow out onto her pillow and she'd get it in her hair. I told her that she wouldn't get it in her hair, because situations like that are where eye crispies came from. When she tried to tell me I was wrong, I asked her if she'd ever heard of hair crispies. The next morning, she examined her eyes in the mirror, and was thoroughly disgusted.

"I can't go to sleep because I can't figure out how the chickens kept their feathers."

"They just did. I'm tired. Let me sleep."

"Well, fine then."

The room would grow silent, and she'd stay true to her promise to not bother me anymore.

But I would fall asleep listening to her ponder out loud.

"How did the baby chickens get in the beehive?"

The house in Huron was the right size for the five of us, but I desperately wanted a dog. We didn't have a backyard, though, so Daddy kept promising me that we'd move out into the country soon and he'd get me a puppy.

I longed for the day that his promise rung true. Then, one glorious November day, Mama and Daddy picked us up from school.

"We found a new house!" Mama said, "It has a big barn and a big kitchen and lots of room to run and play!"

"Can I get a puppy?" was, of course, my first question.

"Not right away," Mama said, "We'll have to

wait until spring, but John- tell her about the barn."

"There's kittens in the barn," Daddy said over his shoulder, grinning. He knew what great news this would be for me. "I don't know how many. There's an old gray and white mama cat and I think I counted six babies in the loft, but I don't know if there's any more."

It was only a week or two before we made the move, and by that time all the baby kittens had disappeared, but the mother cat remained. She was small and scrappy looking with a scar across her face from some cat battle she had participated in earlier in life. Daddy said she was old, at least ten. Carrie named her Suzy. Carrie named everything Suzy.

There was about four feet of snow on the ground when we moved in, and for three little Tennessee girls, the weather seemed bitter cold. We'd never seen anything like it before in our lives. Even living in Huron, the other houses around us had prevented the snow from drifting like it did out in the country. I worried that the sun really could get frozen over the horizon and worried that, after it all melted, our house might float away.

Soon, though, time rolled around for Mama to chauffer Hallie and me into town for our first day of school at Cavour Elementary. As we walked into the building, I thought for sure this was some sort of joke.

To the right of us was a bookshelf, covered in shoes. We walked past it, and around the corner from the bookshelf was a small office, where an older gray-haired man whose name I can't remember sat in a desk alongside a pretty, dark haired woman. Her name was Carol, and I would soon find out her son Christopher was in my grade. I would come to love Carol dearly, and I find that I still wonder about her, and hope she's doing well.

"Hello!" The gray-haired man said, extending a hand to my mother. Mama had Carrie, who was not yet old enough for school, on her hip. I stood on one side of Mama and Hallie on the other. I glanced over at Hallie and could see her looking around the office, as fully bewildered as I. This wasn't a school. It couldn't be. It was way too small. And quiet.

The gray-haired man was the principal, but only that year. The next year, another lady would take over for him. Her name was Sue. I love Sue as much as I love Carol.

The principal took Mama, Hallie, Carrie, and me on a tour of the school. He motioned towards the bookshelf by the door. "These are everybody's outside shoes," he said, "When kids go outside for recess, they stop here and change their shoes before they go outside, then they change them again when recess is over. It keeps the floors in the hallway dry."

"Uh," Mama interrupted, "Are those EVERYBODY'S shoes?" I was glad she asked, because I'd wondered, too.

He chuckled, "There's only about 80 kids in the whole school. This building houses the first grade through the fifth. The kindergarteners have their own smaller building that I'll show you in a minute. First and second grade come in this door. These are their shoes. Third, fourth, and fifth grade come in that door." He pointed down the corridor to another entrance on the opposite end, with another shoe shelf, "Junior High on up is held in Iroquois, about ten miles east of here. They change buses right here in front of the school."

This is craziness, I thought, *she can't really be going to leave us here.* I had put in time serving Kindergarten back in Tennessee and had started the first grade at Washington Elementary in Huron. I knew what a real school was and what it wasn't. This wasn't.

The tour continued.

"Downstairs, you will find my office. Carol is our secretary, and also the school nurse. The bathrooms are also down here, as well as the first grade classroom." He motioned towards a room that had construction paper turkeys taped to the door, each with a name written on its belly. I wondered where they'd put mine, and if I'd get to make my own.

The Principal motioned into another room, across from the first grade classroom, and for the first time I noticed the unusual orange colored marble tiling that the building was floored with. It can only be described as freezer-burned tangerine. The school also had its own distinct smell- like Elmer's glue and grilled cheese with just a sprinkling of talc. That particular shade of orange to this day will cause me to remember that particular combination of smells. The room he motioned to had different flooring, but not much prettier. There were two very large freezers and several folding tables leaned up against one wall. On the opposite wall was another tall bookshelf that held what appeared to be thousands of board games and a box of dodge balls.

"This is our cafeteria, our gymnasium, and where we have our school programs and PTA meetings," the Principal explained. My mother didn't say a word, but I kept watching her. She stood, stone-faced, taking in the information. I was hoping she'd tell him he was ridiculous and take us back home, where she and Daddy would discuss the situation and decide we didn't need school because we were already pretty smart, and could certainly make a good living delivering pizzas.

"I love it," Mama said, "I just really, really love it. I think this is going to be a good school for my girls. They're kind of shy and Jenny has a lot of sinus trouble, but I'm always home just call me if they need anything."

I thought I would choke. I thought Hallie would drop dead. I knew Carrie had pooped her pants. I could smell it, but that was totally unrelated.

The principal shook Mama's hand, and told her he'd get us to our rooms. She walked down the hall and past the shoe shelf and disappeared into the snowy outdoors with Carrie, who had been fast asleep, drooling over her shoulder since the explanation of the second shoe shelf. I looked at Hallie. Hallie looked at me. We were both terrified to be in this funny little town with this funny weather, stuck at this funny little school with these funny talking people.

But there was no escaping. They'd catch us when we stopped to change our shoes.

"Forever is composed of nows."

–Emily Dickinson

My first recess at Cavour Elementary scared me. My class had heard there was going to be a new student, but they had been misinformed and were expecting a boy. When I showed up, the boys were sorely disappointed, and the girls followed their lead. Nobody wanted to play with me that first day, so I wandered the playground alone, looking for Hallie. Hallie, though, had already made a friend and didn't want to be bothered with me.

I found a tunnel on the playground that was built from two large tractor tires and climbed inside. At least it would be warm there, and nobody would see me. I could avoid having to talk to anyone. But I was wrong. Someone crawled in shortly after I did.

At first, I thought about not saying anything to her. Not that she was threatening. She actually looked very sweet. She reminded me a lot of Hallie's porcelain dolls. I just wasn't sure what I would say, and the other kids at Huron Elementary had made quite a joke of my southern accent. I had more or less decided that twelve years wasn't very long and it probably wouldn't be hard to make it through all of my schooling without ever speaking out loud again.

The girl smiled at me, very meekly, through her lavender colored scarf. Her dark bangs hung out the top of her white stocking cap and her purple hood framed what little bit of her face was still visible through all her winter bundling. She had the darkest eyes I've ever seen, but they weren't scary. They were kind.

I smiled back at her and waved, not really sure what to say. She waved back, and we sat there in that tire tunnel facing each other for the remainder of our ten minute recess without speaking a word. When we heard the bell ring, beckoning us back inside, I walked with her. She got into the first grade line, which pleased me. We walked together through the doors and changed our shoes. Then, we took our coats, gloves, and hats off and put them in our little half lockers. Her hair was long and dark and re-minded me of Hallie's. Hallie hadn't cut her hair since she was a very small child, and it was now all the way down to her hips. This girl's hair wasn't as long as Hallie's, but the coloring was the same and it was curly. She smiled at me again.

"I'm Stefanie," she said.

"I'm Jenny," I said.

And for the next several years, the two of us were inseparable.

It was nearing Christmas time, and I still hadn't given up hope of a new puppy. My parents had repeatedly turned down my request by telling me it would be best to wait until spring, so I was taking it to the big man.

Santa Claus always gives kids puppies for Christmas. I knew he wouldn't let me down. I wrote multiple letters and went to the mall twice to remind him. He asked me once in the mall what kind of puppy I wanted and I told him I didn't even care as long as I got one, but then went home and worried that he'd bring me one of those hairless ones that are always at Westminster. I'd never seen any of those puppies in person before, thus leading me further into my paranoia. There had to be a huge surplus of them somewhere. I just knew that's what he would bring me.

During dinner one night, Mama asked us all again what we wanted for Christmas. Hallie and Carrie rattled off their requests, then I told them all that I had already spoken with Santa Claus about a puppy. Hallie glared at me over the red rims of her glasses.

"You know you aren't getting one, don't you?" she asked. Hallie has a certain tone that she's always been able to achieve with her voice to make me feel about ten IQ points short of being a cheese grater.

"Santa said he'd see what he could do," I managed to squeak back.

Daddy looked at Mama, and Mama smiled at me, "Then he probably will bring you one," she said. Daddy grinned and shook the paper straight and turned the page.

"Yea," he added, "Santa's pretty good about keeping promises."

Christmas Eve found us at Aunt Camille's.

With the exception of my mother, Aunt Camille has always been my favorite cook. In the summer time, we would go there and Uncle Tim would grill hamburgers, hot dogs, and chicken breasts. In the colder months, though, we could always count on lasagna or chicken schnitzel. I don't remember which she prepared for us Christmas Eve, but I'm sure it was delicious. It always was.

She had her Christmas tree up, too. It was at least twice the size of ours, and had blue lights and a train that ran its way around the bottom, just like in the movies. I wondered why we didn't have as nice a tree at our house. Hers looked like a display tree at the store and ours looked like it had been decorated by little kids, which it had, but that was beside the point. Why was everything at Aunt Camille's house always so much nicer than the stuff at ours?

I had plenty of time to ponder these things because Christmas Eve drags on forever when you're a kid. When we were little, Mama always took us to Bethel Church outside of Yale for Christmas Eve services. I'd spend all day looking forward to the service because they'd light the church with candles. I loved the sight of that little church lit up by candlelight. I used to imagine that when I grew up and got married, that's how I'd do it- in a little church by candlelight after dark. There was never a prettier sight than that. I also loved the Christmas Eve service because my daddy would wear a suit. He hardly ever dressed up for anything, but when he did, he looked quite cavalier. Mama always cleaned up well, too. On Christmas Eve, I always had good looking parents, which made me very proud. They were like TV parents, and I so wanted to be on TV.

When I'd get to church, though, it felt like we'd never make it out alive. There are always a handful of people that come every Sunday to any church. But then there are those families- like ours- that didn't make it in every week. Everyone shows up on Christmas Eve, though, putting the church at maximum capacity, making it hot and stuffy. I've always been a little uncomfortable in crowds. Even the candlelight couldn't distract me from my anxiousness. My stomach would knot up and I'd feel like I needed to use the bathroom, but I learned when I was about six that it was usually just my brain tricking my body into thinking it had to use the bathroom so I'd have an excuse to escape momentarily. I began ignoring my stomach pains, and was eventually able to ignore them away completely.

The thing about church services when you're a kid is that, as endless as they seem, the end always seems to come abruptly. The pastor would leave the podium and walk down the aisle, and it would always leave me looking around thinking, *Is that it? Is he done? That was quick.* Even though ten minutes ago, I was thinking that I had already been there several hours, and there was no way we'd get out in time to get to bed so Santa could come.

That's the beauty of church. The minute it lets out, you forget how long you've been sitting there. You're so happy to be done, and your soul feels better. The way your brain feels when you finish a good book, or your stomach feels after a piece of warm apple pie, church fills your heart.

Once home from church, there was never time to discuss the service because you had to immediately change into your night gown, brush your teeth, and head off to bed or Santa Claus would see the lights on and not stop. I miss the Christmas Eve mad dashes through the bathroom and up the stairs.

Christmas Eve was the one night of the year that Carrie would fall asleep without argument, but none of us would sleep very long. Hallie was usually the first up. She'd sneak to the living room to see if Santa had come. If he had, she'd come back to get Carrie and I and the usual Christmas morning fight would start. I can still hear her voice, as it sounded then, waking me up.

"Santa came! It's your turn to ask."

"I'm the middle kid, Hallie, they won't listen to me anyway. You're the oldest. They respect you. You ask."

"I asked last year. Get Carrie up!"

Both of us would shake Carrie, "Get up! He came!"

She would lunge to her feet almost instantly, "Are you sure? Did you look?"

"I looked," Hallie would confirm, "But we haven't woke Mama or Daddy up yet. You need to go do that."

"Why me?"

"Because I checked and Jenny's the middle kid."

"Well they're mad at me for peeking at the ones Grandma sent!"

The arguing would continue sometimes for a full hour before we'd either settle the dispute with rock-paper-scissors or we'd hear Daddy's call, "Get up girls. Santa came."

That Christmas, though- our first South Dakota Christmas- I had to ask. Hallie's rock beat both mine and Carrie's scissors, and I was wrong when I assumed Carrie would play scissors again. Her paper covered my rock.

I heard the puppy before my feet hit the bottom step, though, and I squealed.

"I guess they're up now," Hallie heckled somewhere behind me.

They'd already been up, though, waiting for us. "Time to open presents," I heard Daddy tell Mama.

"Well we slept in this year. It's a quarter to five," she laughed back.

They made me wait until everyone was in the living room, then Daddy opened the puppy's crate and took her out. She was so tiny, and- much to my relief- had hair. Beautiful hair. Cream-colored hair.

"It's a little girl Cocker Spaniel!" Mama called out from the kitchen as she made the coffee, without even having seen the puppy yet.

That should have been a dead giveaway for me, but as children we rationalize things we want to believe in, and I wasn't ready to let go of Santa. I just figured that Mama really knew her dogs, and could tell by the yipping.

I named her Lady. Actually, Daddy named her Lady. But I liked it, so I didn't argue.

I don't remember a single other gift I got for Christmas that year. Just that he had done it.

Santa had proven his existence.

I'm sure Lady was not the puppy my mother had in mind when she contacted the breeder. I think she had an idea that, because Lady was little and cute, she'd be sweet. She was wrong. Terribly, horribly wrong.

Lady was vicious. She loved me, but was very territorial. At night, she'd crawl up into my bed and nobody could come in the room without her getting defensive and growling. She was no bigger than my Daddy's boot, but could tighten up her throat and produce a growl that would have a person believing she weighed two-hundred pounds.

It wasn't long before winter opened up into spring, and the little farmhouse really began to come alive. The snow had barely melted away when

Suzy's newest litter made their first appearance. Mama called Carrie and me to the kitchen to look out at the cellar doors. I couldn't imagine what might be so exciting about the cellar until I looked out and saw three of the fattest, fluffiest lumps of cute since Fuzzy's birth four years prior. There was a solid black one that Carrie named Suzy Junior, a gray tiger-striped one that I named Toonces, and a gray and white one that looked very similar to Suzy senior, but for some reason we named HER Oreo. Why the one that looked like Suzy was named Oreo while the black one was named Suzy Junior makes very little sense, but so did many of the things my sisters and I did.

Within a week, Oreo disappeared. Then Suzy Junior. Soon, all Suzy had left was Toonces, and she would stand all seven tired, worn out, bony pounds of her over him as if he were the only kitten left in the universe, and the future of all catkind depended upon his survival. This made him very spoiled and, long after he should have been weaned, we would hear him crying out for her from the barn. All baby animals from humans to chickens get the same desperate tone in their voice when calling their mother. Mama would be outside hanging clothes on the line, sometimes, and we'd hear Toonces off in the distance let out a worrisome cry and Mama would yell back, "Get it yourself! Mama's tired!"

I would wonder if she realized she was yelling at a cat or if, perhaps, she had only heard the tone and not the cry itself. Sometimes I felt like just maybe I should point out that it wasn't me, just in case later on her memory failed her and she found herself annoyed with me for no good reason.

Suzy wasn't the only one on the homestead with a new bundle to swoon over.

Fancy, my Mama's cow, was expecting and due at any moment.

Mama always loved to do things the hard way. While we lived in Dairy country, with big commercialized farms and equipment all around us and a gallon of milk cheaper at the local convenience store than anywhere else in the world, she wanted to have her own cow and milk by hand. So Daddy bought her a Jersey cow from Helen and Gail, two women that operated a dairy farm outside of Tulare, South Dakota. They brought Fancy to Mama, and she had Daddy fix her own milking parlor in our little barn, complete with a stool and bucket. She bought a one-gallon pasteurizer and a one-gallon hand churn and saved milk jugs for weeks before the calf was born. I don't know how much milk she thought she was going to get out of one cow, but the woman had plans and that was evident to everyone around her. She could hardly stand the excitement in the days before Fancy gave birth. You would have thought she was getting a new grandchild.

But the night of the birth was horrifying.

"Fancy had a girl!" Mama had called out from the doorway, having just gotten back from refilling the water in the barn, "A great big girl, too! You girls get ready for bed. I have to go move the calf." Since

Mama was planning to milk Fancy, she had been advised to put the calf in its own stall in the barn and bottle feed it calf starter. That's the part that excited me- feeding the baby bottles. Mama had told me that would be my chore, and it gave me a great sense of importance.

We put our pajamas on and jumped into Mama's bed. We weren't going upstairs until Mama made it back in and told us about the new baby because we were, possibly, more excited than she was. It wasn't long, though, until Mama came busting in through the back door again. Daddy's coat hung off her shoulders and she was fumbling to get her work gloves off her hands as she reached for the phone. She had on some old faded blue jeans and one of Daddy's t-shirts stuck out from under the coat. If it wasn't for her few blonde curls sticking out from under her stocking cap, she could have easily been mistaken for a man. And a very angry one at that.

She had her jaw clenched and her face was red, either from the cold or her fury at what she had discovered when she went back to the barn. The three of us waited in silence, knowing better than to ask her right now what had happened. We listened intently, hoping to pick up the story from her half of the phone call. When the phone was picked up on the other end, she didn't even bother saying who she was, she just cut loose.

"Your dog was in my barn! He's limping because I kicked him. He chewed the ears off my new calf!" Without further explanation, she slammed the phone down, picked it up, and began dialing a second number.

We weren't able to tell who she was talking to during the second call, either Helen or Gail or maybe a veterinarian. But they instructed her on what to do about the calf and she headed back out the door again- crying. We were left on the bed, still waiting to find out what would happen with the earless baby. We could hear the television in the living room announcing a winter storm warning. They didn't need to warn us- we already knew it was going on. The blizzard was obvious when we looked out the windows.

Eastern South Dakota blizzards are nothing short of amazing. The land is flat and there are few trees to hold back the wind, so the snow blows sideways. At times, it doesn't even look like it's hitting the ground. It just blows sideways and seemingly back up into the sky. My Grandma Sybil used to have a snow globe that sat on top of her television and when we'd go see her in the summers I'd shake it, trying to figure out a way to show her how a South Dakota blizzard looks, but no matter how hard I'd shake the thing I couldn't get it right. There was never enough snow.

Even as a little kid, when my arms couldn't have been longer than a couple dozen inches, I'd hold my arms out straight and not be able to see my hand from the blowing snow. And the blizzards always ended as abruptly as they began. One minute you wouldn't be able to see out the front door, then the next minute the snow would seemingly stop blowing in midair and all of it would float peacefully to the ground, as if to say "That's enough now, I'm done dancing. Let me rest."

I worried Mama was cold out in the barn. Lady had picked up on the agitation in the house and had become volatile. She had us cornered onto Mama's bed and would bark if we tried to get off of it. I think she knew something terrible was happening outside. Maybe she was trying to protect us by keeping us in her sight. Whatever the situation, though, we were terrified of all ten pounds of her.

The phone started ringing and we all knew it was Daddy. It was his time of night to call and he had no idea that the calf had been born then mutilated by the neighbor's dog or that Mama was outside in the middle of a blizzard or that all three of his littlest girls were being held captive by an irascible stocking stuffer.

"Someone has to tell him what's going on," Hallie called out, "Jenny. It's your dog."

She was right. It was my dog, and my duty to do something about the situation. "Lady," I called, "Come here girl!" Maybe if I acted like I wanted to play, Lady would forget commandeering the situation while our mother was outside, powerless to protect us.

Lady's tail wagged. This was a good sign. The phone was still ringing in the kitchen. Also a good sign- Daddy hadn't given up yet. I reached down to pick Lady up, and nearly had my arm ripped off. I'd never heard her snarl like that before. She wasn't herself. She was either very sensitive to the tribulations of the moment, or a doggie sociopath. Or maybe a little of both.

The phone stopped ringing. Hallie sighed.

"Daddy's going to wonder where we're all at," she said.

Carrie looked worried. "We're never getting off this bed, are we?" she pouted.

I thought I'd try to ease both their minds. "He'll call back and Mama will tell him what happened. And Mama will be in soon. When she comes in, Lady will stop. I think Lady's just nervous."

Hallie, as a child, could be very dramatic. My perfectly reasonable statements didn't satisfy her. "What if Mama freezes to death out there?" she asked. Carrie gulped back tears.

"Mama's not going to freeze to death!" I yelled, "She's got on Daddy's heavy coat."

"Have you looked outside, Jenny? It's bad. Really, really bad!" she replied. I was about sick of her at this point and couldn't resist the urge to be snide.

"If Mama froze to death, then Daddy will be home in a few days. If I die first you can eat me."

"I'm tired," Carrie whined, either having ignored everything I'd just said or trying to interject and stop a fight.

"Good thing we're in a bed, then, I guess, huh?" I snapped back. Hallie had done it now. I was angry.

"Why don't you just shut up?" Hallie screeched,

"She's little. You don't have to be mean like that."

"YOU shut up!" I yelled back, "You're the one scaring her talking about Mama freezing to death and stupid shit!"

They both gasped, then, Hallie looked smug, "I'm telling."

We'd been here before. This was nothing unusual. I knew what to do. I grabbed a handful of Hallie's hair and wrestled her down to the bed. "Say it," I said.

"No!" Hallie yelled out in defiance. I pulled back on the hair a little more.

"Say it!" I yelled.

"OKAY! Shit!"

I released Hallie's hair. She couldn't tell on me for saying "shit" now because she, too, had said it. Carrie leaned up against Mama's head board, grasping Kermit to her chest. She had a stuffed Kermit doll that she carried everywhere with her. She even vowed to marry him when she grew up. Kermit was the replacement for Teddy who had been disfigured in a horrible incident involving a teething coonhound.

"If you tell on us we're going to throw Kermit away," Hallie warned.

"Okay," Carrie nodded.

Never underestimate the wiles of little girls. They all play dirty.

The phone started ringing again and Lady started barking. All of our fighting had distracted Lady from her siege and the ringing phone had caught her off

guard. This was our one chance. I leaned off the side
of the bed and managed to get a hold of her red
rhinestone collar. "Run, Hallie, I have her!" I called
behind me.

Hallie leapt from the bed and made a run for the
kitchen where she was able to grab the phone on only
the third ring. It was Aunt Camille. I listened as
Hallie cried and recounted the horrors of the evening.

I held Lady back as she continued to bark at
Hallie in the kitchen. Finally, Mama walked in the
back door again. Lady instantly quieted down and
laid at the foot of the bed. She knew she was no
match for Mama.

"Who's on the phone?" Mama asked.

"Aunt Camille," Hallie said as she handed the
phone over. Carrie and I crawled off the bed and
walked into the kitchen to listen in on the conversation.

Mama told Aunt Camille about the situation in
the barn and we learned then that Fancy's baby was
going to survive. She just wouldn't have any ears,
but Mama had stopped the bleeding and had decided
to name her Jolene. "Camille, I've got to go," Mama
eventually said, "I'm getting a beep and it's probably
John."

Mama pulled the phone from her ear and
punched the flash button.

"Hello?" she answered, then almost instantly
looked annoyed. "We've been right here! Hang on..
Girls? Why didn't you answer the phone when

Daddy called the first time?"

All three of us began yelling our separate versions of Lady's rampage. Mama put her hand up to silence us, sighed, and continued.

"Every dog in Beadle County's gone crazy, I guess. You're not going to believe what happened in the barn tonight.."

*"The world breaks everyone, and afterward many
are stronger at the broken places."*

–Ernest Hemmingway

Despite her obvious wickedness, I loved Lady. I loved it when the weather finally warmed up enough so I could bring her outside to play. I loved to run with her around the barnyard, chasing Toonces and Suzy and I loved it when we'd go into the barn to see Fancy and earless Jolene.

Mama had chickens, too, and in the spring time she would let them out to roam the barnyard and Lady would look at them, aching to chase just one for just a minute. And, sometimes, if Mama was inside and I knew she wouldn't catch us, I'd let Lady run into the flock, breaking up their group. She got as much good out of the excitement of the scattering as she would have if I'd actually let her catch one, and I have to admit it was pretty funny for me, as well.

Lady didn't much care for the neighbor's Labrador because he was bigger than her and always wanted to play rough, but she'd wag her stubby tail and give him a friendly yip hello when she saw him and be on her way to find some other smaller animal to torture. When Mama would decide we needed to run into town for groceries or an appointment or some other task, Lady would be taken inside to wait until I could come home and play with her again.

One morning, though, we couldn't catch Lady to put her inside.

"Just leave her outside," Mama said, "She'll be okay until we get back. We need to go get some tomato plants." Mama was working on getting her garden ready to plant, and I was excited to help her that year. Because of my excitement, I agreed to just let Lady stay out. I wanted to hurry up and get to the greenhouse in town and pick out what I wanted to plant in my row.

The greenhouse in Huron was one of my favorite places when I was a child. Carrie and I liked to walk through and pretend we were exploring the jungle. Mama would let us play in the greenhouse as she looked outside for the plants she wanted, then she'd call to us and we'd find the man in charge and pay him for what Mama had decided to take home. Even then, I would wonder how this man stayed in business and how many people left without paying. He seemed very trusting, and my mother was certainly a very honorable lady for not just stealing the tomato plants despite the opportunity.

As we pulled onto the little gravel road heading

home, I asked Mama "Are we going to plant these today?"

"We might," Mama said, "We need to get all the laundry done first, because.." her voice shook, then she was quiet for just a second. She started slowing the car down. "Jenny, don't look," she warned, "look at the floorboard. Don't look outside."

I did as Mama asked and stared at my feet. I heard her open her door and get out of the car. When I was sure she couldn't hear me, I looked up at Hallie, who had not been told to look at the floorboard and was at that moment watching Mama and asked, "What's outside?"

Hallie didn't even hesitate. "Lady got run over," she explained, "She's dead."

I couldn't resist the urge to look. As I turned, I saw Mama kneeling at the side of the road, Lady laid out in front of her. Mama picked Lady up and moved her further into the ditch, then walked back to the car and got in. She looked back to find me still looking at my puppy, and tried to comfort me.

"She's smiling. She never knew what hit her."

It wasn't good enough, though. I felt my heart twist and tears came flowing from my eyes. I had never hurt this badly before, and I knew there was nothing that could be done to stop the pain.

"When Daddy gets home, we'll see about getting you a new puppy, if you want."

"I don't want a new puppy," I said, "I just want to go to my room."

"Okay," Mama said, "Go on. We'll plant the

tomatoes in the morning. You just go lay down. I'll bury her by the barn, okay?"

"Okay," I choked.

Mama looked for something to comfort me. "What do you want for supper tonight? I'll make anything."

"I don't want anything."

"Daddy will be home tomorrow. He's going to Wicks Auction. You love Wicks Auction."

It was no use. I just walked up the stairs to my room. She didn't understand. Nobody understood.

My best friend just died- and it was my fault. I didn't care about the garden anymore. Or Wicks Auction. Or what we had for supper. None of it was worth Lady and if I hadn't been so excited over stupid tomato plants, she would still be okay.

I laid in my bed and listened as Mama told Hallie to watch Carrie while she buried my dog. I felt like I should go outside and help her, but I couldn't bring myself to do it. So, instead, I laid in my bed and cried myself to sleep, knowing I'd have the chore of waking up all on my own.

This time, there would be nobody to lick my face good morning.

Daddy returned from the road the next day as promised. He made it home in the early morning hours before I woke up. I was awaken by the smell of their morning coffee and his first cigarette of the day, and immediately thought of Wicks Auction. I knew I said I didn't want to go the day before, but was hoping Mama would understand that I'd changed my mind. I loved Wicks Auction.

I crept downstairs to find Daddy and Mama sitting in the living room. She was sitting next to him on the couch with her head on his shoulder and it was obvious in her eyes that she'd been crying. This made me want to cry, too. I choked back the tears and said "Good Morning."

"Good Morning, Baby," Mama smiled through her own sadness, "How are you this morning?"

"I'm fine," I said, suddenly remembering that I had not eaten my dinner the night before, "I'm hungry, though."

"I bet you are," she said, beginning to stand up, "What do you want? An egg in the hole?"

Egg in the hole was my Mama's specialty. She would use a glass to cut a hole out of the center of a piece of bread, then butter both sides of the bread and the circle piece that she had cut out. She'd fry them both in a pan, dropping an egg into the hole in the center of the bread. None of her children could resist them.

"Yea," I said, "And cocoa?"

"Okay. Sit down with your Daddy. I'll fix it for you."

I crawled up on the couch by my Daddy and rested my head on his arm, just as Mama had been doing, except I wasn't copying her. I always liked to sit like that with my Daddy.

"I'm sorry about your dog, honey," Daddy said, patting my knee.

"Yea," I have never known how to answer condolences. You can't say it's okay because it isn't. But if you say anything else, it looks like you want the attention which I never did. "Mama said you're going to Wicks Auction today."

"I thought I might go see what they've got," he chuckled, "You want to come with me?"

I don't know why he bothered asking. He already knew I did.

Wicks Auction was among the seven wonders of my small world. It was located just south of Cavour and people from all over the state would haul their junk there three or four times a year to sell. Whatever you wanted, you could find it there.

The outside of the building would be scattered with rows of farm equipment ranging from antique tractors that didn't run anymore to new equipment, barely used. There were tables set up with boxes of household items that people didn't need anymore. There were usually a few sheep or pigs in a pen somewhere in the yard and maybe even a cow or two.

Inside, you could find old furniture, appliances, racks of clothing, and cages of rabbits and chickens. Once in a while, a chicken would escape and an older man- I assume one of the auctioneers- would tell all the children at the auction that if they could catch it for him, he'd give them five dollars. I never was able to catch the chicken, but it made for great fun anyway.

Someone at the auction always brought their dog. I never knew the dog's name, but he was some sort of border collie mix and very well fed. He was as wide as he was tall, and very friendly. Kim, a girl from my class at Cavour, was always at Wicks Auction. Her grandfather always had things he sold there, and she would always come with him. Kim and I never played much at school, but we'd find each other at Wicks Auction and have great fun looking in at the rabbits and chickens and petting that old dog.

Because people came from all over to sell at Wicks Auction, there was a wide assortment of kids at the auction, too, and other than Kim I never knew any of them. They were always friendly, unlike some of the kids I rode the school bus with. I suppose the difference was that their parents were at Wicks Auction and not on the bus, and it wouldn't be hard to get in trouble if you weren't careful.

Getting yelled at by your parents was the worst trouble a kid could get into at Wicks Auction. Everyone there was friendly and nice and it was perfectly safe to let us go play, even as young as six and seven years old. All the Daddies, and what few Mamas came, would go off to look at equipment and just let us run free. Nobody was going to hurt us or try to take us. Nearly everyone there knew each other, and a few old ladies would sit in the lawn chairs and keep an eye on us all. If we got too close to the road or started wandering too far from the auction yard, someone would yell for us to come back even if they had no idea who we were. Once, a little boy was chasing a runaway chicken and fell, scraping up his knees and legs. One of the old men picked him up and carried him inside where an old lady cleaned him up, then the two of them carried him through the crowd to find his mother. People just looked out for each other's kids.

Cavour, South Dakota is unlike any other place on earth, I imagine. Wicks Auction is still in business, and I like to think it's the same way now as it was then. Sometimes I think it might be nice to make the trip there with my own children sometime to find out, but I fear it won't be and the disappointment will be more than I can bear.

Lady had only been dead a couple weeks when tragedy struck us again.

Mama had called us all outside with her to help plant some seeds in the garden. It was a beautiful day out. Suzy and Toonces sat perched on the dumpster, watching us plant. The neighbor's Labrador walked sat in the middle of the road, watching them and hoping for a chase. Fancy was in the barn lot grazing and even Jolene was soaking up the sun through the wire fencing as she waited for her afternoon snack.

Carrie was sitting in the dirt beside me, sulking because she'd been brought outside. I was using my finger to poke holes in the dirt to drop the seeds in.

"I don't even like vegetables," Carrie protested. I turned to find her burying Kermit in the dirt- one green foot and his big plastic eyes were all that was left sticking up out of the earth.

"You're going to get him all dirty," I nagged. I wanted to be outside planting seeds. I was planting cauliflower and had big hopes for my crop.

She grabbed his one free foot and pulled him out. The dirt ran off his body and down his face, some into his mouth. He looked hot and miserable.

"See?" I asked, "Now Mama's going to have to wash him."

Carrie held Kermit up at her eye level, his back against the sun and frowned. "Mommy!" she called, "I'm taking Kermit inside! You have to wash him for me!"

Mama gave Carrie the look. The one that says, "Okay, but this is it. I've about had it with you." She put one hand on her hip and used the other to wipe the sweat from her brow before pointing at the door.

"You take him inside, but you come right back out here. I'm not going to play these games with you today."

Carrie loved to stall when she was a little kid. Once, when she knew bath time was coming, she purposely spilled a bag of rice on the floor and set to work picking it up, one grain at a time.

Carrie hopped up out of the dirt and ran to the house, still holding Kermit by one leg. He flapped in the air behind her. She was only inside for a minute, then ran back outside.

"He's on the washer, Mama," She called out.

"Okay," Mama said, "Now come put some seeds

in these holes for me.

Carrie did as Mama asked. Hallie had was working on her own row, and the four of us spent the next half our or so planting seeds and talking about Daddy. Then, Hallie stopped and looked at the house.

"Did you guys hear that?" She asked. I had heard it. Something broke inside the house. Something glass.

"I think a plate fell," I said, "We should go see."

Mama rolled her eyes. She hadn't heard it. "Just finish planting these seeds and we'll be done. Quit stalling."

"Something really broke," Hallie protested, obviously insulted that Mama didn't believe us.

"Well we'll see it when we're done," Mama snapped back. Knowing better than to keep arguing, we kept planting, ignoring what we'd heard. But soon Mama saw it, and it couldn't be ignored any longer.

"Oh my God!" She called out. She dropped the onion bulbs and started running towards the house. "Y'all stay here. Don't come in!"

Black smoke was billowing from the kitchen windows. An occasional flame danced behind the glass. Mama opened the back door and more black smoke rolled out as she disappeared inside.

The three of us stood in the garden, facing the house, waiting for her to return. "If she doesn't come out soon, I'm going in," Hallie explained, "But you guys just stay here, okay?"

"Mama said not to go in," Carrie said, "Don't. She'll be back."

We watched the house a little longer. Hallie started walking, hesitantly, towards the back door. She didn't make it far, though, before Mama reappeared.

Mama ran out the back door, clutching Kermit to her chest. "Go to Marvin's!" She yelled.

She spoke too soon, though, because Marvin had already seen the smoke and was on his way over from his house, which sat just up the road a little bit from ours.

"Pull the car away from the house," he yelled at Mama, "I've called the fire department."

I was watching Mama back the car away from the flames when Fancy caught my eye.

Fancy paced by the barn, keeping an eye on Jolene. Even though she was no longer responsible for the daily activity of caring for her calf, she was worried for her safety. Suzy called for Toonces and they ran towards the barn together. I could hear my mother every few minutes call to us, "Stay right there. Don't come any closer to the house!"

All the mothers on the farm shared the same desperation.

I heard the fire truck's siren coming from way up the road. I didn't think it was going to stop as it rounded the driveway and a few men jumped off.

The fire department in many small South Dakota towns is volunteer, meaning the firefighters get called in from home when something like this happens. One of the firefighters was wearing a tie, having obviously been somewhere much nicer only moments ago. Despite the obviously bad timing, Carrie and I couldn't help but laugh at the sharp-dressed fireman as he unwound the hose on the back of the truck. Hallie glared at us, though, and our laughter subsided.

I felt a hand on my shoulder and looked up. Marvin, his face covered in soot, furrowed his brow and patted my head. "You guys climb in the back of my truck," he said, "I'm going to drive you to my house. Ruth will get you all something to eat. I'll come back and get your Mama."

We did as Marvin asked, knowing Mama wouldn't mind. Mama trusted Marvin and Ruth, and they trusted her. There was already a small crowd accumulated at Marvin's when we got there- mostly the wives of the firefighters having come to watch their husbands work from a safe distance. When we walked in the back door, several of them scurried to make us sandwiches and tell us how everything would be fine. They asked where our Mama was, and we told them she'd stayed at the house.

"Go get her," one of the ladies said to Marvin, "She doesn't need to stand over there and watch it go down."

I hadn't realized until that point that "going down" was exactly what it was about to do. We were going to be homeless. We already were. Everything we owned was gone, except Kermit.

He was the one thing Mama grabbed as she left

the house. It wouldn't have been wise to go upstairs and the fire had already engulfed the kitchen. If she was going to save anything, it had to come from the living room or her bedroom and the one thing she grabbed was Carrie's Kermit. He meant more to her than anything of her own.

The ladies kept us from the windows until Mama came. They didn't want us to see. When Mama got there, she called Aunt Camille who came right away. The fire trucks were still at the house when we drove by on our way to Huron and Aunt Camille's house and rest. Carrie and I wore Timmy's pajamas that night, but the next day we had clothes of our own. Mama had gone while we were in bed and bought a few things, and some people from the church had donated others. Daddy was on his way home, too, having finally gotten the message about what had happened.

Marvin sold insurance and was working with Mama to get a settlement from the insurance company so we could get our lives back to normal. Mama and Daddy decided to buy a pre-manufactured home and move it back onto the land so that we wouldn't have to change schools again, but it would be at least several weeks before we could move home. They had to clean up the mess from the old house and dig a basement for a foundation before they could move the new house in.

Mama and Aunt Camille had gone to the store and left the five of us children with Uncle Tim when Hallie and I finally got a chance to talk alone.

"Have you ever noticed Daddy's always gone when bad stuff happens?" She asked.

I had, actually. But it was no fault of his own. He had to work. And he always came home right away and helped do what he could.

Mama just had ridiculously bad luck.

_____

"A rock pile ceases to be a rock pile the moment a single man contemplates it, bearing within him the image of a cathedral."

-Antoine De Saint-Exupery

Mama and Daddy rented a small efficiency cabin from the Westview Motel in Huron while we waited for our new home.

The Westview Motel also found its way onto my Seven Wonders list. The motel itself is hidden on the far West side of Huron off of third street, and could be easily mistaken for a summer camp, with its circle driveway and 1920's-era cabins. At that time, an elderly couple managed the hotel and had a produce stand set up outside the main office. We were assigned cabin three, which Jean, the manager, explained to us had once housed sheep. Evidently, some rancher from Montana had wanted his animals to sleep in comfort. She told us to let her know if we encountered any problems and left us there to get comfortable.

The cabins were nothing spectacular. Ours had two beds, a bathroom, a television, and a small kitchenette. It was certainly close living quarters, considering the three of us girls were having to share a bed and Mama and Daddy were only sleeping three feet away, but Mama said we'd make do for a couple weeks. Some ladies from the church brought over several board games for us to play, as well as more clothes and blankets. Daddy got his paycheck from the trucking company, and Mama took us to the grocery store to stock our kitchenette.

The first few days we were at the Westview, we occupied ourselves with the board games and watching MTV, which we didn't get at home. Then, we started becoming restless. Jean came to Mama's rescue, though, when she invited us to play on the playground she and her husband had built for their grandchildren behind the main office.

Along with the playground, Jean had planted a beautiful flower garden with a path all the way through it. Colorful flowers decorated the yard and once in a while there was a ceramic frog or gnome to greet us. We would have played in that place all day, if Mama had let us, pretending to be lost in some enchanted world. But it was a hotel, and there were too many strangers for Mama to let us stray far for long at a time.

Daddy set to work getting us a home back. The insurance company settled, and he was able to buy the modular home and enough furniture to fill it, as well as pay a company to dig a basement and pour concrete. Once the mess from the fire was cleaned up, Mama and Daddy would take us with them when they'd go back out to the property to work.

The barn and all the outbuildings had survived the fire. So did the animals. Suzy and Toonces watched the progress from the roof of the garage and the cows were bellowing every time we turned in the driveway to be fed.

All the smoke, rain, and digging had brought out the toads. One of the contractors had two sons, close to mine and Carrie's ages, and they'd come out to the property with their dad and help Carrie and I catch the toads and put them in a bucket. We'd spend all day capturing them. Then, at the end of the day, we'd let them go again. That way, we'd have something to do tomorrow.

After days of searching, we caught the queen mother of all toads. Suzy was the first to spot him. She had started teaching Toonces how to catch smaller animals. She was an excellent mouser and, understandably, wanted to pass on this talent to her son- and what better to train with than a yard full of slow-moving amphibians? When she found "Frog-zilla" as he was soon named, though, she was a little bit terrified and her screeching caught the attention of Carrie, the boys, and I.

He was easily as big around as a saucer and probably weighed two pounds. It took both my hands to hold him, and when we put him in the bucket, he could jump, extending his back legs, and nearly reach the top.

"How old do you think he is?" One of the boys asked.

"Probably fifty or sixty years old," said the other.

"Where do you think he came from?" Carrie chimed in.

"His mother, I guess," the second boy answered. He had all the answers.

"What are we going to do with him?" I asked.

"Keep him in the bucket a while and then let him go," he answered again. Through all his answering, the tone in his voice never changed. While the rest of us were hardly able to contain our excitement over the amplitude of polliwog in our bucket, he remained strangely unimpressed. I wondered about his life, and what unspeakable things he must have seen.

We watched Frogzilla hop in the bucket for a few minutes before deciding he was taking up too much room. We freed him, he hopped under the garage, and was never seen again.

I imagine he's probably at least forty pounds by now.

The day finally came when the basement was complete, the plumbing was run, and it was time to move in the house. Daddy and I followed the truck as it hauled our new home to the property. I couldn't wait to be able to move in. After spending a couple weeks in a small efficiency cabin with my parents and sisters, I just knew that our new house would seem huge. Mama and the other girls rode in the car behind Daddy and me.

Once there, Mama, my sisters, and I waited and watched as the house was secured to the foundation. When it was time, Daddy waved us over to go inside.

Our living room was big, and had a fireplace and a bar that connected it to the kitchen, which had a dishwasher. Mama had never had a dishwasher before. I was excited for her. Off of the kitchen was a hallway, which led to the laundry room, a bathroom, and two bedrooms. Hallie would once again get the small bedroom, while Carrie and I would share the larger. Mama and Daddy's bedroom was right off of the living room, and they had their own bathroom and a walk-in closet. There was also a mud room at each door, where we could kick off our shoes when we came inside.

Soon, Daddy moved the furniture in. Because of the size of our bedroom, Carrie and I had to share a double bed, which made the nighttime Legend begging even more fun, but it was nice having her there in the winter, or when we'd watch a scary movie against Mama's recommendation.

By the time school started, we were settled in again, and Mama had hatched a new plan.

"Respect is about how to treat everyone, not just those you want to impress."

-Richard Branson

Mama decided she needed a job of her own. Hallie and I were in school and Carrie would be joining us soon, then after that she'd have nothing to fill her days with. She was also interested in learning more about the dairy business and Helen and Gail needed some assistance. All the pieces fit.

So while Hallie and I were in combat all day against the savages of the playground, Carrie joined Mama at work on the farm.

Helen and Gail raised Jersey milk cows. Jerseys are the smallest of the milk cows and have the highest fat content in their milk, making them ideal for butter production. Most dairy farmers in South Dakota prefer Holsteins, so to see a Jersey farm was quite a novelty.

The breed of the cattle on the farm wasn't the only obvious difference between Helen and Gail's farm and others in the area, however. In fact, the most often discussed difference had nothing to do with the cattle at all, but who raised them.

Helen and Gail were both women. They were also a couple.

I didn't realize, at first, that they were what they were. They both dressed in jeans and flannel shirts and kept their dark hair cut short. Gail wore glasses and, while they both had feminine voices, it was easy for a seven-year-old to mistake Gail's voice for that of a soft spoken man, which is what I assumed she was until I referred to her as "he" and my father corrected me.

Then, it only seemed logical that the two of them were sisters. Why else would two women live together into adulthood? I was in the barn with my daddy, checking on Aretha, Mama's new pregnant cow, when I finally decided to ask.

"Are Helen and Gail sisters?" I blurted out.

Daddy was pacing in the barn, already, but he paced just a little faster after I asked. He always paces when he thinks. He looked at me and took a long drag to finish his cigarette, threw it on the ground and smothered the butt with his boot. Exhaling, he answered, "No, I think they're just friends." He, of course, knew better and was merely avoiding having to get into a lengthy discussion about sexuality with his little girl.

I wondered if Stefanie and I would live together when we grew up. I really hoped so. It would be fun to live with your friend. Every night would be a slumber party. Stefanie and I had discussed growing up many times before, anyway, but it had never crossed our minds to live together- only what we were going to do when the authority of our parents had exhausted and we were left to our own devices for the remainder of eternity. We would never make our beds again, and we'd have McDonald's whenever we wanted, and when we got home, we'd watch nothing but MTV and VH1 and eat frosting from the can. We'd have at least half a dozen dogs each and huge tanks full of tropical fish. There would be no need to do laundry, we'd simply buy new clothes every day. But we would never smoke, drink, or do drugs. That was uncool. And we would only have boyfriends that didn't want to kiss or see us naked. That was gross, and we didn't understand why anyone would ever want to be with someone so demanding.

The thought of our future boyfriends led me to my next question.

"Do Helen and Gail have husbands?" I asked. I would have asked if they had boyfriends, but I guessed they had to be at least in their mid-20s. They should have been married by now.

"No, I don't think so," Daddy answered immediately. This one didn't require as much thought as the first, I could see.

"Do they have kids?" I asked. I'd never seen them with kids before, but my friend Samantha's mom wasn't married, so maybe Helen and Gail were single mothers, too.

"No," Daddy sighed, "They don't have kids, either. They have their dogs. Their dogs are like their kids."

Helen and Gail had two dogs named Angie and Astro that went everywhere with them. Even when they'd run to the store, the dogs would ride along and wait in the truck. This was another of mine and Stefanie's plans- we'd keep at least one dog in our car. Dogs in cars at grocery stores seemed like so much fun.

Daddy stood and looked at me as he lit another cigarette. I could see in his eyes that he was thinking hard about something. He took a long drag as he stared at the loft stairs, then exhaled. The smoke billowed from his mouth and nose and up into a hole in the roof of the barn that led to the loft.

When he saw me staring up into the loft, he couldn't resist smiling. He had thought of the diversion from "20 Questions: Lesbian Edition."

"Did you know Suzy's pregnant again?" He chirped.

I couldn't believe it. This was fabulous news, but I had to be sure he wasn't just teasing me.

"Nuh-uh," I said, "Toonces isn't even a year old!"

"Cats don't have to be a year old," Daddy laughed, "Old barn cats like Suzy can have two or three litters a year."

This was even more fabulous news. I imagined that before long, we'd be overrun with fat, fuzzy kittens. And nothing was more beautiful than that.

"How do you know?" I asked. My daddy's infinite animal wisdom amazed me. He could have been a veterinarian if he wanted. I just knew he could have. He had never gone to college, though, and had settled for trucking, which he had done since he was just a teenage boy. I never understood why he didn't go to college. He was very smart, and I had no idea about money until I was much older.

"She's making a nest in the loft," he said, "And she's been moping around screaming at Toonces for days to leave her alone."

The first part made me happy. I was excited for new kittens. I just felt so bad for poor Toonces. He was being replaced, and it wasn't long ago that Laura had broken the news to me about Carrie. At least my Mama still let me live in the house, though. Poor Toonces was all on his own.

In all actuality, Toonces was well over the acceptable age limit to still be living off his Mama. For a cat, anyway. He was nearing a year old, and had grown from a fat little kitten into a tall, muscular tomcat. He had learned well from his mother, and had become an excellent mouser. He had even defended her against that dumb Labrador a time or two. But, he was still a kitten in his soul. He still wanted to cuddle up to her at night. He still cried for her when he couldn't find her in the barn lot. When Mama would take the cats a bowl of dinner scraps, Suzy still backed off and let him eat first. Now, he had been thrust out into the world like a sack of garbage. Poor, poor Toonces.

I decided I needed to find him. I left the barn and went on a search, calling his name. He wasn't in the shed, or at the chicken house. He wasn't in the back room of the barn, and he didn't come when I yelled up into the loft. He wasn't in the garage, either, and I couldn't get under the house. I decided to walk back further into the barn lot. Towards the back of our property, by the tree line, there were some old concrete culverts that weren't buried, but stacked on top of each other. What they were doing there is anyone's guess. They came with the property when Daddy bought it. There was also an old junk car. It was some sort of rusted out, swamp green contraption from the 1950's. It no longer had seats and was missing one of the doors.

I found Toonces hiding inside.

Toonces was tame, unlike many of Suzy's other children. She had a habit of hiding her litters so well that they didn't get much human interaction, making them feral. Toonces was about six weeks old when Carrie and I caught him, and it was as if he knew instantly that we wouldn't hurt him. When the other kittens would continue to run and hide from us, he wouldn't. This had actually once led our mother to believe he was sick, so she had a talk with us to prepare us for his imminent death. He was the only surviving kitten in his litter, though. The other two were claimed by either hawks or their father- an insanely huge yellow tabby-striped tomcat that only came around once every few months to visit Suzy and impregnate her, insuring he would have more victims on his next visit. He was brutal, and we all hated him. He once attacked Carrie for no good reason, leaving claw marks from her knees to her ankles. When Marvin saw Carrie's injuries, he vowed sanction, citing the cat claw marks on his dog's face as even more excuse to keep his gun loaded. To my knowledge, Mama never told him Toonces was actually responsible for the latter of the crimes.

Although Toonces was tame, he still didn't like being picked up. I reached in the broken out car window to pet him, and he leaned his head against my hand and purred. I stopped petting and called him to come out of the car so I could reach him better. He crawled out and rubbed against my leg, so I decided to sit on the ground and spend a little time with him. I made myself comfortable, cross-legged in the grass and looked for Fancy. She was busy grazing, and had no interest in trampling me. Jolene was locked in a separate pen and Aretha was in the barn. I was safe. I rubbed my fingers through the fur on Toonces's back. His hair was very short, even for a cat, and felt like the rough half of a Velcro shoe strap. His stripes were beautiful, unlike most tabbies I'd seen. Rather than just being straight across his back and down his legs, they swirled. His face was long, like his mother's. Some cats have round faces, but not Toonces or Suzy. Their eyes sat close together on their faces, giving them the dignified look of a lion. There was nothing cute about either of them. Some cats spend their whole lives waiting for someone to pick them up and cuddle them. Not the ones that lived in our barn, though. Our cats meant business.

Every day except today, anyhow. Toonces was aching for a little attention today. He crawled up into my lap and rolled onto his back, asking me to scratch his belly. His purring was so loud, I could hear it over the rustling of the wind blowing through the trees, and I could feel the vibration of his purring on my lap.

"It will be okay," I comforted him, "You're a good cat. Carrie's not so bad. You'll get used to it."

Just then, Mama yelled for me from the back door. It was time to eat. Toonces was skittish, and the unexpected sound of my mother calling my name prompted him to jump from my lap and climb a nearby tree.

"Bye, Toonces," I waved, "I'll see you later or maybe tomorrow, okay?"

Toonces didn't even bother meowing at me as I walked away. He just watched, wondering why I had to go and who would love him now.

It rained that night, and I still worry about whether or not he kept warm.

A few weeks passed. Suzy had her litter and they all fell to local predators, so Toonces was once again her pride and joy. Only now it was worse. She had taken to trying to pick him up by the scruff of his neck, as she had when he was a baby. Since those days, he had grown to nearly twice her size, however, so her attempts at babying him were quite the sight to behold.

Aretha had a boy, Fancy was taken back to the dairy to be impregnated a second time, Jolene kept growing, and I decided that I, too, wanted a cow. Mama had a handful- why shouldn't I have at least one?

Stefanie raised a Holstein calf every year for 4-H, and it always seemed like such fun. 4-H is a youth organization that can be found in many rural communities that is set up by the United States Department of Agriculture. The 4 Hs stand for "Head, Heart, Hands, and Health," with the official 4-H pledge stating, ""I pledge my head to clearer thinking, my heart to greater loyalty, my hands to larger service and my health to better living, for my club, my community, my country, and my world."

In 4-H, there are several projects that a child can undertake, ranging from arts and crafts to raising livestock. In raising livestock, a child can raise chickens, rabbits, sheep, goats, pigs, horses, or cattle. Stefanie's dad worked for a Dairy Farm outside of Cavour, so his boss always allowed Stefanie to raise one of their Holstein calves for show. I wanted to compete with Stefanie, but not against her. The fact that my mother and Helen and Gail all had jerseys made this possible. Because my calf and Stefanie's calf would be in two different breed classes, we could compete alongside each other, and neither of us would have to outdo the other. It was the perfect plan. But with Jolene being earless, she would have been disqualified and Aretha's son wouldn't work for obvious reasons. It would be months before Fancy had another baby. I had to persuade my mother to get me a new girl calf.

This proved surprisingly easy. My mother loved the idea of me joining 4-H, being as cow-crazed at the moment as I, and immediately talked to Helen and Gail about a baby for me to raise. They picked out one of their pregnant cows and promised me her baby, but she delivered a boy, which delayed my start a little while longer until a girl calf was born. Within a couple days, they brought her to my house and set her up in a calf hut by the garage.

She was beautiful, and she was all mine. We named her Annabelle.

Annabelle seemed very small to me, but it was only because Jolene had been so ridiculously huge. Annabelle was the perfect size for a Jersey calf, and, very soon, was outgrowing her calf hut. With 4-H Achievement days drawing near, it was getting close to time to halter-break Annabelle for the show. This meant wrestling a halter onto her, and leashing her to a fence post to get her used to being led. While tied to the fence post, we'd bathe her with the hose, and brush her, and even clip her hair. The notion of show cows is something that I know sounds very silly to most people, but it was serious business to Stefanie and me. Her calf was named Daisy, and was much farther along in the halter breaking process than Annabelle. Stefanie was a pro at this, however, having competed in the calf shows the previous year.

I decided I needed her help, so I told Mama that a weekend sleep over was in order. Mama agreed, and Saturday found Stefanie and me at the barn talking cow.

"Annabelle's really pretty," Stefanie said, petting my cow's black face. Jerseys are all brown in color, but sometimes there will be brown ones with white patches and sometimes a calf's face and neck will get darker as they age. I always loved black-faced Jerseys. They look smarter, somehow. Annabelle, though, was clearly not smart at all.

"I like Daisy, too," I replied. Stefanie and I had a brilliant friendship that consisted of returning every compliment with a compliment. We had only been mad at each other twice, and both altercations ended with someone getting physically maimed and a tearful apology, only to be forgotten the next day.

Stefanie's parents were born and raised on Pearl Creek Colony near Huron. They were Hutterites. Hutterites are a communal branch of Anabaptists that have colonies set up throughout most of the Dakotas, as well as other rural areas nationwide. They learn English and German both from birth. Their colonies depend mostly on farming or ranching, and are virtually self-sufficient. The women wear long dresses and bonnets, but their attire is unlike the Amish in that they are allowed to wear colors, and quite often do.

Hutterites are also pacifists, which led to the torturing of several during World War I when they refused to go fight the war. Many were imprisoned in

Leavenworth where two were ultimately killed.

I never knew exactly why, but Stefanie's parents, Margaret and Larry, had decided when Stefanie was very small that they didn't want to raise her on the colony, so they left and started a new life on their own. Because of their colony upbringing, Stefanie was a very disciplined child. Even as young as seven years old, it was not unusual for us to find her hanging laundry or doing dishes for her mother.

Stefanie's parents were not cruel or tyrants, by any means. They were very sweet, loving people that welcomed all children into their home with open arms. I used to love spending the night at Stefanie's house. I found her mother interesting, and I loved to watch Stefanie's father pick at and tease her. She was her daddy's girl, just like I was mine.

When Stefanie would get in trouble, her mother would scold her in German to keep me and any other houseguests from knowing what she was saying. Sometimes, Stefanie would yell back at her mother in German. It seemed strange to me that someone as young as Stefanie and I were could be completely fluent in two different languages.

At the time of Annabelle and Daisy, Margaret was pregnant with a second daughter.

"I wish my mom would hurry up and have the baby," Stefanie said, "She's been grumpy."

"Yea," I said, "My mom gets grumpy, too, sometimes. It'll be okay. Little sisters aren't so bad. I always have someone to play with."

All of this, of course, was a big lie. My sweet

little Fuzzy had grown into a toy-thieving, candy-eating, Mama-hogging, tattling monster over the last several years. She was fun to play with once in a while, but all our games ended the same way. She wouldn't like the rules and she'd go cry to Mama that I wasn't playing fair, which led to Mama being grumpy most- not some- of the time.

Stefanie just nodded. She didn't believe me. She knew me too well. But she didn't want to call me a liar, either. It was best to let the baby sister conversation rest. She, instead, reached for Annabelle's collar to show me a trick.

"If you hold her halter right up here by her chin, she can't get away from you as easy because even though you aren't very strong, she'll feel like you are."

She was a wealth of bovine information.

I looked at Annabelle, and where Stefanie was holding her halter at her chin, "So if I have one hand on her chin, then how do I hold the lead rope?"

"You hold her under her chin with your right hand," Stefanie clarified, "And you hold the end of the lead rope in your left. That way, if she gets her chin away, you still have a good hold on her because of the rope."

I looked at Stefanie, then Annabelle, then the halter and the lead rope tied around the fence post. It was time. I was going to try to lead her through the yard.

Mama had warned us several times about untying Annabelle when she wasn't there to assist, but I didn't care. I thought it would be a marvelous surprise for Mama if I were to just lead Annabelle up to the window and knock for her to look out and discover that I had done it myself. I reached for the knot in the lead rope and started unraveling.

Stefanie was worried. "Maybe we should get your mom," her voice quivered.

"It will be okay," I said, "I can do it. Just hold her chin."

Stefanie reached up with both hands and held on tight to Annabelle's chin as she watched me untie the lead. When I had a firm grip on the rope, I put my hand up by Stefanie's and found the ring in Annabelle's halter to hang onto.

"I got her," I said, "You can let go now."

Stefanie kept hanging on. She looked at me, worried, not wanting to.

"Are you sure?"

"Yes!," I yelled, "I've got her. Just like you said. Let go!"

Stefanie did as I told her, but the result was not what I expected.

The weight of Stefanie's hands leaving the halter gave Annabelle the false impression that nobody was holding her anymore. Not wanting to be apprehended again, she took off running and my finger was caught in the loop of her halter. She wouldn't have gotten far, but I had untied her from the fence post, allowing her to run for miles if that's what she wished.

I felt for certain my finger was broken. It hurt

terribly. I was fortunate, though, because having one hand stuck to her halter kept me from falling down flat on the ground. Instead, I was running backwards alongside Annabelle, wrestling with the halter to free myself.

A young heifer can run much faster than a child, though, so I was tripping and dragging my heels in the dirt the whole way. I just knew she was going to run dangerously close to a tree and I'd be dead. I could see Stefanie running behind us. Having gone into panic mode, Stefanie was now expelling a rather long string of undecipherable German expletives. Every once in a while, she'd lunge forward in an attempt to grab Annabelle's tail, causing me to yell "Stop! She'll kick you!"

"I'm going to go get your Mom!" Stefanie sobbed.

"NO!" I yelled back, knowing how much trouble we'd be in.

"She's going to kill you, Jenny!" Stefanie cried, "I have to!"

Finally, Annabelle stopped. She had grown tired from all the running and laid down to rest. Stefanie pounced, holding down her head while I freed my fingers, which had now turned to a deep shade of purple.

"Are they broken?" Stefanie cried.

I felt them with my good hand. They had gone numb from being stuck, but I could bend them. "No," I said, "They're just sore."

"How are we going to get Annabelle back?"

Stefanie asked.

"Maybe if you hold one side and I hold the other she won't run again," I said, fearing Stefanie would say no. Having witnessed what she had just witnessed, I wouldn't have blamed her.

But Stefanie was a better friend than most.

"Okay," she said, "Let's get her to stand up."

I reached for Stefanie's hand and pulled her up. Annabelle stayed lying in the grass, watching us, almost daring us to try to make her move. Stefanie, being the more cattle-savvy of our pairing, stood up first and grabbed Annabelle's halter under her chin at both sides and leaned back, pulling Annabelle to her feet.

Fearing Annabelle would take off running, only this time dragging Stefanie, I grabbed at her halter with both my hands to hold her. This is where Stefanie got the idea.

"If I walk on one side of her and hold her halter with both hands and you do the same, she won't run," she paused between thoughts, and then decided she needed to clarify, "I don't think so, anyway."

I didn't think so, either, but I also knew that if we were wrong, we'd both be pulled this time, so at least we would go together. As we walked towards the house, I realized my pants were ripped and my knee was bleeding. Stefanie noticed, too.

"What are we going to tell your Mom?" she asked, worried we'd be in serious trouble, I'm sure.

"I'll think of something," I said.

Mamas sense things, though. And my Mama had

already come to see what she was feeling.

"Why don't you just tell me the truth?" I heard her say. Stefanie was as startled as I was. We were busted.

I looked up to see Mama, standing at the end of the yard staring us down, her arms crossed in front of her. She was mad.

I started crying. Stefanie started crying. We were going to have to come clean. Before either of us could speak, though, Mama uncrossed her arms.

"How bad are you hurt?" she asked.

"I scraped my leg and my fingers are bruised," I said.

"Stefanie?" Mama asked, "Are you okay?"

"Yes, ma'am," Stefanie answered.

Mama took Annabelle's lead rope and we let go. We watched as Mama drug her back to the fence post and tied her. Mama was beautiful, but always tough. Once, I had heard someone- I believe Gabe- refer to her as "one part thoroughbred, two parts mule." Whoever it was, they were right. Mama was tough, and stubborn, and worked hard for everything she had. But she was also soft, and beautiful, and carried herself with more dignity than anybody I ever met. Stefanie and I had blatantly defied her. Then, even after knowing we had done so, she overheard us conspiring to lie about it. And she caught us red-handed. It was stupid and dangerous and we could have both been seriously hurt. If it weren't for my fingers getting caught like they did, I would have been drug across the ground- maybe killed. It would not have been out of line for her to punish us for what we had done.

But we weren't seriously hurt. And that's why she didn't.

Instead, she waved us inside. She put me on the counter and cleaned up my knees and gave me ice for my fingers. Stefanie sat in a chair and watched, waiting for the inevitable. We both knew Mama would tell Margaret, and then after Stefanie got picked up and taken home, we'd probably each be punished separately for what had happened.

"It was my idea, Mama," I tried to explain. I didn't want Stefanie to be in trouble.

"Hush," Mama said, "It's alright."

I heard her tell me to hush, but I wasn't ready to, yet. This would prove to be a lifelong problem of mine. "She didn't even want to; I told her it would be okay. It was all my fault."

"Jenny!" Mama yelled, "Hush!"

It wasn't long until Margaret returned for Stefanie. By that time, the two of us were sitting on the couch next to each other in the living room, silent, both dreading the moment.

My mother answered the front door. Stefanie and I both held our breath, listening, waiting to hear what would be said. But nothing was said other than the usual "Hi! How are you?"'s that take place between the parents of childhood friends.

Together, they walked into the living room, where Margaret immediately spotted my knees and the ice pack on my hand.

"What happened?" her thick German accent echoed through the living room.

I didn't speak. Stefanie didn't speak. Finally, Mama laughed and said, "Oh, the calf got carried away and drug Jenny a little bit."

"You have to be careful with those cows," Margaret told me, "They'll kill a person."

And that was it. No yelling. No spanking. No forbidding Stefanie and I to play anymore. They just dropped it completely.

My hands and knees healed within a couple weeks, Annabelle learned to lead and took home a blue ribbon that year. That glory faded with time, too.

Just about the only thing that did remain was the memory of our mothers on that day, and their lesson in compassion.

"Sticks in a bundle are unbreakable."

-Kenyan Proverb

A t the homestead, it wasn't uncommon for our cable to decide to fuzz out during adverse weather. When this would happen, we'd be left with only local channels and channel thirty seven, which was some blasphemous station out of Atlanta of all places on which several people sat side by side all day in golden thrones talking about the love of God and how, if everyone watching would send them a monthly contribution of one hundred dollars, they could cure anything from Downs Syndrome to AIDS through the power of prayer.

One of the women on the show, much to her own dismay, was not Tammy Faye Baker, although she tried to dress the part. Her make up was outrageous, even making the golden thrones look modest. Her dresses were even more flaunting. Despite having the face of a very over-adorned nursing home resident, her hair was dyed yellow. Not blond. Yellow.

And it tinted orange under the studio lighting, which may have been the reflection of the chairs. I don't know. I never will.

Because of this one individual's attire and the ridiculousness of the furniture, my sisters and I loved to watch them and laugh. We, of course, never turned our noses up at religion. Our parents raised us as Christians and even as children we believed in and loved God. But nobody could resist the giggles that came with this particular broadcast and, on a rainy day, there wasn't anything better to do anyhow.

On one particularly rainy Saturday, Mama had gone to the dairy. She normally didn't work on Saturdays, but for some reason this particular time, she did. With her gone, the three of us girls spent much of the morning fighting over the Super Nintendo before we all tired of video games and decided to watch television. Because of the weather, all we could find were cartoons, which we all liked to pretend we had outgrown, and the religious fanatics on thirty-seven.

Truth be told, we would have all rather watched cartoons, but our pride and the knowledge that Mama would be in soon to make us turn the channel drew us to channel thirty-seven instead. We had to get in our laughs while we could.

We watched for about an hour, then Carrie asked Hallie if she could go to her room and listen to music in Hallie's CD player, which was quite the novelty in those days. Hallie agreed because she was going to take the phone into Mom's room and call Catherine.

I stayed in the living room, watching the crazy lady on the religious channel, who at that time was telling some contemptible story about a one-legged baby in Guatemala that sprouted a second leg after an investment banker in Boston sent in a cash donation in his honor. This story caught my attention because I was secretly wondering about getting Jolene some new ears.

She opened up the phone lines and started taking calls from people worldwide. People were calling in, rattling off their ailments and she would put a cash price on how much it would cost to cure them through prayer, because some ailments require more prayer than others, I guess. The first lady called in with nearsightedness and was quoted fifty dollars. The next lady's uncle had lung cancer. She paid fifteen hundred dollars right away.

Mama came in as the phone was ringing with the third call. She sat in her chair to relax and read through the mail as I continued watching my show.

The caller was sobbing and telling a tearjerker of a story about how her son is going to burn in the fiery pits of Hell because Satan has taken hold of him. I assumed he'd killed someone, the way she was carrying on, but then she revealed that he was gay.

"Mama," I asked, "What's gay?"

Mama hadn't been paying much attention to the television. "It's when a boy loves other boys or when a girl loves other girls," she explained, "Why?"

"Because this lady on TV's son is gay," I answered.

"Oh," she replied, half listening as she read over the phone bill.

Equipped with the knowledge of what "gay" meant, I was even more intrigued. I'd never really heard of the concept of someone loving their own gender before. In fact, I didn't think it was possible. I didn't think I'd ever seen such a thing.

Until I realized I had.

I started thinking about Helen and Gail and wondering if, maybe, this was their situation.

I knew I should turn the channel. I knew my mother didn't like me watching this one, and continuing to watch it with her sitting in the same room was dangerous. But I had to learn more. I had to know.

"He's bound for Hell," the sobbing mother on the phone said, "I can't let him be around my other children because I don't want that kind of influence on their lives."

The overly-made woman looked sympathetic as she began asking questions.

"Ma'am," she asked, "How do you know he's committed these acts?"

The woman on the phone sniffled and sucked back tears. "He told me."

There was a united gasp among the throned evangelists. The Tammy Faye postlude was brought to tears and could no longer speak. An older man took over for her.

"This is going to require quite a bit of prayer," he began, "Many have been blind sighted by Satan into believing this is biological and that a person can't help it. A true Christian knows that is merely an excuse for the morally perverted to justify their disgusting acts. Homosexuality is a crime against mankind introduced by the devil himself and the Bible, itself, states that all homosexuals shall be put to death by stoning. We can't do that in the present day, but I need your assurance that, if he is resistant to prayer, you will not let him pull your other children into this ungodly lifestyle."

"I promise," the woman sobbed, "I have to think about my children first."

But HE is your child, I thought, *What about him?* It must be a terrible feeling to not have a mother that loves you.

"Many homosexuals are so far into their sin that we can't save them," the man explained, "but we will try. It will take all of us and several more. I can put your son on the prayer list for a thousand dollars down today, Ma'am."

I still don't know if she paid him. My mother turned off the TV.

"God doesn't take MasterCard. And it doesn't matter if you're sitting in a throne or on the crapper, he hears your prayers and your prayers are enough. You don't have to pay other people to do it for you," Mama voiced.

I was a little surprised. I didn't think she was paying attention. I had to say something so she knew I wasn't some sort of religious monomaniac. "I know," I nodded, "I just watch it for the chairs."

Mama nodded as she drank the last of the water from her glass. "I know that," she said, setting the glass back on the table, "I'm not stupid. But I want to tell you something else."

She paused, probably trying to figure out her wording. Then she looked me straight in the eye and grabbed my hand, squeezing it. Mama was queen of the hand squeeze. That one simple action was all it ever took for her to allow any of us to feel exactly how much love she had for us. There was a warmth that would start in your hand as she squeezed and spread all throughout your body. Like she was giving a little bit of her life to you. Maybe she was.

"If there's a Hell," she half-whispered, "And I believe there is.. Nobody gets there by loving someone. God spoke one time. Everything since then has been commentary and if you're a good person and you see the good in other people and you love everyone as they deserve to be loved, then you've lived a good life," she pointed at the TV, "Those people have no idea what they're talking about and they can't bring anybody closer to God. God is something everyone has to find on their own and no matter what anyone tells you about being baptized or having babies before you're married or who you love in this world I just want you to remember that the only thing that will for sure keep us out of Heaven is hate."

I knew, now, that it was okay to ask.

"Are Helen and Gail…" I didn't know if I should say the word. "Gay" might be something bad. Like the "N" word to black people. In all the lecturing, that had never been clarified. I just left it at "Gail" and hoped she'd know what I was getting at.

Mama nodded, "Good people. Helen and Gail are good people."

It had been more than a year since Lady's passing when death would come knocking on our door a second time.

It was a Saturday morning when Carrie broke the news to me. I had been at Stefanie's overnight on Friday, and my mother didn't tell me when I called home to tell her good night. I assume she didn't want to upset me at the sleepover.

Carrie was busting at the seams with big news as I climbed in the car for Mama to take me home.

"Can I tell her?" she looked at Mama and asked.

"Go ahead," Mama sighed.

"Toonces is dead!" Carrie yelled, almost gleefully- she never got to share big news.

"What?" I was stunned, "How?"

"He got fried!," Carrie answered. There was a twinkle in her eye. This was a big moment for her.

"Fried? Mom! How did Toonces get fried?" I was thoroughly confused.

Mama looked back over her shoulder, "Marvin's stupid dog," she said, shaking her head, "He chased him up the telephone pole."

This had to be a joke. That was the dumbest death I'd ever heard of. Toonces had more brains than that. And he'd taken on the dog before.

"You're kidding," I said. She had to be.

"No, honey," Mama said, "Daddy buried him this morning. He was outside smoking and watched it happen."

I couldn't believe that Toonces's life had ended so abruptly. And strangely.

"How's Suzy?" I asked. Mama grinned.

"Oh you know Suzy," she said, "She's just like any of us. She'll pick it all up and move on."

Mama was right. Suzy did. Within a couple months, she was fat again with a new litter. The first snowfall had arrived, blanketing the prairie and drawing out just a little extra bit of good in everybody.

Margaret, Stefanie's mother, was getting close to delivering her baby. Christmas was only around the corner. Daddy had switched trucking companies and could now be home more often. Things were looking up and starting to get exciting in my quiet corner of the world. And, the day before Thanksgiving, I had no idea how much more exciting it was about to get.

I was happy to be on my way home. Thanksgiving break had officially begun. Once I had endured the bus ride, I was free for four whole days, and tomorrow Mama was cooking a turkey.

Public school buses are among the most horrid places on earth. Ours was one of the worst.

There were few seats where a child could sit and feel safe and even if you felt safe, it didn't mean you were. There were several eighth-grade thugs that rode the bus with us that felt the need to pick on the younger kids for absolutely no reason other than their own amusement. If a younger child tried to stand up for themselves, they were picked on even worse. If someone stood up for somebody else, they might as well be committing suicide. I learned fast and I learned early to not talk to anyone. Instead, I sat quietly in my seat and tried to look out the window or read a book. Anything to keep from making eye contact.

Our route was so terrible, we went through about a bus driver a semester. Nobody kept us very long. At one point, we had a driver that assigned seating by writing names on masking tape and marking the seats. Brian, one of the worst bullies, was seated next to me. Except his nametag didn't have his real name on It. The bus driver, who must have suffered from some form of dyslexia, had instead written "Brain." The most troublesome part of this for me was that Brian didn't seem to notice. He just sat in his seat and never spoke a word. Nobody else seemed to notice, either, except me and I didn't want to be the one to point it out. I would either be murdered by the eighth graders for noticing what they hadn't, or I'd be taken under their wing for pointing out our driver's faux paus. In either case, I'd be heading for trouble.

I learned a lot on the school bus, though, by listening in on their conversations. The closer I could manage to sit to the back, the more interesting the conversations became. This is where I learned how to cuss, what tampons were, and several verses of the diarrhea anthem.

It's also where I did a lot of thinking. One day, I got so lost in thought that I fell asleep. When I woke up and recognized that I was near my home, I couldn't remember if I was coming home from school or on my way there. I didn't want to ask anybody and look like a fool, so I crossed my fingers and hoped I was on my way home. Imagine my disappointment when I realized I wasn't.

But, this Wednesday, I was on my way home, and happier than I had been in weeks. We were expecting a house full of people for dinner the next day, and I loved it when Timmy came to my house to play.

I was so excited to be home, in fact, that I didn't see the surprise waiting for me when I came in the front door. "You didn't see it?" Mama asked as I took my coat and boots off in the kitchen.

"No. See what?" I asked. I was very confused. I didn't know what she might be talking about.

"Look on the basement stairs railing," she smiled.

I walked back by the front door where the basement stairs were located and looked down to see a small calico kitten staring back at me.

"She's a girl," Mama said, "Helen says all calicos are girls. I never knew that. Did you?"

I didn't know. But I was stunned. Where did she come from? Suzy was just pregnant yesterday. It couldn't be hers, and all the barn cats at Helen and

Gail's were wild. Mama wouldn't have brought one of them home.

I guess Mama could see that I was confused, because she answered my question without me having to ask.

"Someone kicked her out in front of the dairy farm," Mama explained, "Helen and Gail found her covered in mud so they cleaned her off and kept her in the milking parlor until I got there today because they thought you might want her. They were afraid the other cats would kill her."

I did want her. I was very surprised.

"Can she live in the house?" I asked Mama, concerned about the yellow cat and the hawks that always got Suzy's babies.

"I guess so," Mama said, "but the litter box is your job."

We named the kitten Patches and she became a permanent fixture of our family. Her contributions were great. She was my pillow when I was sick, a friend to lean on when I was sad, Mama's alarm clock, mouse hunter extraordinaire, and comic relief. Carrie and I invented a secret life for Patches in which she had a torrid love affair with a Persian named Furrio and was lead guitarist in a rock band called "Chicken," thusly named for her favorite flavor of canned Alpo. When she tired of Furrio, she moved onto stalking Garfield, even having a restraining order put out against her.

In reality, though, we weren't far off. She detested all other animals of every species, but she did like music. Her favorite song was "Pink" from Aerosmith. Mama never believed us, but Patches would come running to sit near the stereo whenever we played that one song, then she'd leave when the song was finished. Mama said we were silly, but we weren't. Patches was.

Patches would not be the only animal to enter our lives that year, though. The following spring, Daddy took us to get a puppy from an ad in the paper. He was half blue heeler and half springer spaniel. We named him Sparky.

Sparky was more Daddy's dog than anything, though. He got hit by a car when he was six months old and had to have surgery to fix his shoulders. They put titanium plates and pins in him so he would be able to walk again, but then he grew afterwards, and I believe outgrew his hardware. The cold South Dakota winters were hard on him, too. Because he stayed sore, he had a very short fuse. He was also very protective of all of us, especially Carrie and I. We were the youngest and I think he felt a sense of duty to our father to make sure nobody bothered us. At first, it wasn't a problem, but the older and taller he got the more uncomfortable his shoulders became. He would even growl at our mother if she looked at him the wrong way. He once got a hold of a chicken and Mama yelled for him to let it go. He did, but only because he wanted to snarl at her.

Mama told Daddy several times that his dog growled at her. She even went as far as to say he tried to bite her a few times. Daddy, whose heart beat for

Sparky, would always wave it off. "Aaaw, Mama," he'd say, "Sparky wouldn't bite anybody. He just likes to act big."

Other than Daddy, though, we were all a little scared of Sparky. When Mama was expecting company, she'd have me go get him and tie him by the barn. He wouldn't growl at me, most of the time. I guess I was enough like Daddy.

When Daddy was home, Sparky followed him everywhere- sometimes a little too closely. Twice, Daddy ran over him with the tractor. Already made of steel, Sparky came out unharmed both times. A third time, Daddy stopped the tractor and was immediately taken aback by Sparky whining and howling in pain. He looked down to see Sparky standing close by the tractor. Upon closer inspection, Daddy realized he'd parked on Sparky's toe.

Sparky also liked to ride in Daddy's pick up. He'd sit in the bed of the truck and let the wind sweep through his hair. When riding with Daddy one day, I witnessed what may have been Sparky's most notorious act of gracelessness. As Daddy turned down a gravel road headed home, several ring neck pheasants were in the road ahead of us. They flew to the sides of the truck to avoid being hit and Sparky, desperately wanting a taste of one, leapt forward- mouth agape- hoping, I guess, that he had somehow been blessed with the ability to fly. Instead, he hit the ground, face first, and rolled into the ditch. I was sure he was dead. Daddy started slowing down.

"Where'd he go?" Daddy asked.

"Into the ditch," I said.

Before Daddy could stop to turn around, though, he emerged from the tall grass and started running towards us in the road- trying to catch up. His mouth was still wide open, with his stupid dog smile spread out across his face.

Daddy sighed and shook his head, "Well.. Ain't he a Thomas?"

"Oh yeah," I giggled, "He's a Thomas."

"If you step on people in this life, you're going to come back as a cockroach."

-Willie Davis

T imes were good in the Cavour house. For us, anyway.

Mama didn't like living there. She wanted a bigger home, where all her girls could have their own bedrooms and she didn't have to hear any noise from grain bins. She wanted to live where she had more privacy and less of the neighbors Labrador.

When Daddy would come home off the road, he and Mama would make time to go for drives by themselves. In the Spring of 1995, I had just turned eleven. Hallie was thirteen and Carrie was eight. It was safe for them to leave us home alone while they went for drives, often looking at old houses or farms and it gave them a chance to talk without the interruption of three girls.

One day, they were gone for what seemed like a pretty long time. When they returned, Mama had a certain glow to her. She was very excited and immediately got the phone book out, looking up the phone number for the Clark County, South Dakota court house.

"What's Mama doing?" one of us had asked Daddy.

"Oh, she found an old house she likes. You know Mama. She's nosy and wants to know who owns it."

This was terrible news for me. I didn't want to leave Stefanie. "I'm not moving," I said, as sternly as my eleven-year-old voice would allow.

Daddy rolled his eyes. "Nobody's moving," he said, "Mama will forget all about it in a few days. You know how she is, sometimes."

But she didn't forget all about it. Several weeks later, in fact, she had purchased not only the house but eighty acres around the house. The move was on-as soon as we fixed the place up.

The first time Daddy took us all to see the new house, he warned us that it was not ready to be moved into yet. We were expecting the condition of the house to be bad, but we knew we had about three months before Mama's planned moving day, so it would be okay. I dreaded the move, and leaving Stefanie behind, but I knew I had no choice.

You see, my mother loved old things. Old cars, old furniture, an old man..

When Mama and Daddy first drove us to the house, it was even worse than we had imagined it would be. The grass was grown over the front steps. There were tree branches down in the yard. Windows were broken out and barn swallows had made their nests throughout the house, leaving a thick layer of bird droppings all over everything inside.

The top of the old barn was leaning off of its brick foundation and there were skeletons of chickens all over the chicken house. Who leaves their chickens when they move, anyway? The whole thing seemed really creepy to me, and I was hoping this was an elaborate prank. Maybe we weren't moving after all. Surely my parents hadn't gone completely insane, although they had always teetered on the verge of it.

Mama was ecstatic, showing us where she was going to put the sofa, the dining room table, and a couple spots in the yard she had designated for flower beds.

We were kids, though, and lacked vision. We weren't very enthused at the idea of moving in, even if Mama and Daddy were planning on fixing the house up. It seemed impossible, and even if they did get it to a livable condition, we didn't see how it would ever feel like a home. We liked the house we were living in, where we were within bike-riding distance of friends and we had grown to love Cavour Elementary and our classmates. We saw absolutely no reason to leave behind the home we'd been living in to move into this dump. It just didn't make any sense.

Mama, knowing I was the most adamant about not wanting the move, took me by my hand and led me up the narrow, filthy staircase. She wanted to show me my room.

I followed her to a short hallway, where she turned to her left and motioned into an open doorway.

"See? It's huge!" She had shrieked.

All I saw was a dead raccoon in the middle of the floor. I rolled my eyes and walked away from her.

Mama and Daddy never had a lot of money. They worked hard and gave everything they had to their children. I was too young and ignorant to know at the time that this was more than just a house to my mother. It was everything she'd always dreamed of, but didn't think she'd ever have.

It was also more than a house to my Dad. It was the one promise he had made my mother in their younger days, before all of us, that he was able to follow through with.

So, we set to work on the house the next day. Daddy hired a contractor named Walt to help put on a new roof and popcorn the ceiling, while Helen and Gail offered assistance, as well. This was happening, whether any of us girls wanted it to or not. We figured out it was best to just accept our fate and brace ourselves for a long summer, followed by a difficult move.

Daddy, Sparky, and I traveled to the house alone one day to get rid of the bird nests so Daddy could install new windows and get to work on the cleaning. We waded through the overgrown grass and made our way into the front door to be immediately greeted by the chirping of a house full of baby birds.

"We'll do the upstairs first," Daddy said, tugging my shirt to follow him. Together, we walked up the stairs and into what would be my bedroom. Six nests hung from the ceiling. Daddy walked along the wall, placing his hand in each, pulling down the ones that didn't have babies in them.

"What about the ones that do have babies?" I asked. I knew the birds couldn't stay in the house. I just didn't want them to die.

"That's why we're doing this today," Daddy said, "They're all big enough now to fly out on their own. That's what we're going to do. Show them how to fly."

Surely he was joking. I had no idea how to fly. He grinned at me and walked from my room into what would be Carrie's, then Hallie's. Soon, he had every empty nest on the top floor torn down. It was time to teach some babies.

He reached into one of the occupied nests and pulled out a baby bird. It didn't look so much like a baby anymore, though. It had grown into its adult feathers. It squirmed in his hand and hopped, flapping its little wings. He carried it to my open window and tossed it out. I started to yell- afraid that he had tossed the baby to its death. The bird dropped a couple feet, then took off in flight towards the tree-line.

"Just like Mama does it," Daddy laughed. Daddy whistles through his teeth a little when he laughs, which makes everything he says and does a little funnier.

"Is that how they teach them?" I asked, surprised once again at my Daddy's vast animal knowledge.

"Yes, ma'am," Daddy whistled through is teeth again, "They just kick them out of the nest, and the babies start flying. They already know how by the time their feathers come in, they just need someone to make them do it."

He reached back up in the nest and grabbed the last two babies out of it and handed me one. Nervously, I walked to the window. I pet the little bird's head and prayed it would be as smart as the last one. I didn't want MY bird to be the one that couldn't fly. I would never feel the same about Daddy again.

I sucked in air and held my breath as I tossed. My bird fell a couple feet, just like the last, then found its wings and soared even higher and faster towards the barn than its brother. Daddy tossed his, and it did the same.

I was excited now. Together, Daddy and I ran throughout the entire house clearing nests and teaching birds to fly. There must have been thirty birds that flew from those windows that day. It was the greatest fun I'd ever had, and made me happy I had come along with Daddy that day.

The next phase of restoring the house was cleaning up the bird mess, which Daddy didn't let us help with- he was afraid it would make us sick, then sanding down the kitchen floor to lay new tile.

Once the bird messes were gone, Hallie and Carrie set to work helping Mama and Gail upstairs with the painting. I decided I'd rather learn how to sand the kitchen floor. Helen and I worked on that floor together every day for about a week, sanding away the black tar left behind from the century-old linoleum that had covered it. Helen did most of the work. My little arms weren't able to put a whole lot of force on the sander. But I hung with Helen. I liked doing it. It gave me time to think as I sanded and it kept me from going into the hot upstairs to paint with the other two. At the end of the week, Gail told me I was "tenacious." I didn't know what that word meant, so she explained that it meant I stuck with things. I liked it, and vowed to use the word "tenacious" at least once a day for the rest of my life. This goal fell along the wayside within a couple weeks, though, when Mama got annoyed and told me to quit saying it so much. After that, it started feeling like a bad word, and I didn't use it again for years.

It wasn't long before Mama and Daddy had the old house looking good. The hardwood floors and woodworking that divided the living room and dining room were surprisingly undamaged and polished up nicely. In fact, the hardwood floors throughout the entire house were amazingly unharmed from years of abandonment and weathering. The little kitchen was painted black and white and looked very cute once daddy laid the checkered tiling.

Daddy took us all to the hardware store to pick out new area rugs for our room and told us to pick whatever color we wanted. I picked an off-white beige color. Light colors are my favorite in home furnishings.

On moving day, Helen and Gail once again assisted by hauling furniture in their cattle trailer, saving Daddy the trouble of renting a truck or hiring a mover. Once the furniture and cows were moved, Daddy took my sisters and I back to retrieve Patches, Sparky, and the chickens.

We couldn't bring Suzy. She was half-wild anyway and had started disappearing for weeks at a time. Daddy just knew that the old barn in Cavour was where she had been born and raised and if we took her with us to the house in Willow Lake she would never stay there. She'd wander off and get killed. She had fended for herself for years before we came along, and now she would fend for herself again. She stood in the open loft window and watched as I carried Patches from the house and put her in my Daddy's truck. Daddy had taken a cage to the henhouse to gather the chickens, and Sparky was sitting in the back of the truck, waiting for his ride.

I climbed in the truck and held Patches close, watching Suzy look down from the window.

I was so sorry to leave her there. I was so sorry to leave everything there. Only moments before, I had been in the basement of the house, getting Patches's litter box ready to go. The basement was unfinished and had cement walls that my sisters and I had drawn on with sidewalk chalk many times before. On one wall, we had traced our bodies. The tracings were still there, years old by now, but I remembered doing them. We looked so small.

Carrie's name was written in various places,

always with backwards "r"s. That's where I'd taught her to write her name.

A hopscotch board sat on the floor, and "H.T. + J.B." sat in a heart. Jonathan Brandis. Many an episode of "Seaquest" was watched in that house.

And maybe there would be many more episodes watched there, too. But not by us. We'd spent our last night in Cavour. I'd never wake up in my old room again, and this would be the last time I ever watched Suzy look down on her kingdom from the loft window.

I knew she'd survive. I wasn't afraid of that. I was worried about what I would miss. No more kittens. There weren't any feral cats at the Willow Lake house and Patches was spayed.

I remembered Toonces and Lady and the night Jolene was born. All the excitement that little barn had held, and now it sat empty and quiet and uncertain about tomorrow or what might fill it in the years to come.

Sort of like me.

"School is a drill for the battle of life. If you fail in the drill, you will fail in the battle."

–Karl G. Maeser

The little town of Willow Lake, South Dakota is every bit as charming as its name.

The town is so well hidden that, outside of girl's basketball season, nobody really gave it a second glance. In fact, only people who lived there noticed that the population signs weren't matching. Coming into town from the west, we had a city population of 317 people. If you came in from the east, however, there were 376.

I often wondered which sign was newer. Had the population dwindled or grown? I never asked. Nobody would have known anyway, most likely.

Unlike Cavour, though, Willow Lake had their entire school system in one building. Everyone from kindergarteners to seniors had class in the same place and shared a gym and cafeteria. Because of this, arrangements had to be made, of course, to protect the little kids from the high school stampedes between bells. It wasn't uncommon to see kindergarteners hugging the walls as a group of nearly-grown students ran by.

Overlooking the town is a purple and gold water tower with a picture of a pirate on it- the school mascot. Willow Lake was, and I imagine still is, a community built upon farming. Everyone there seems to raise some or all of four things: corn, soybeans, livestock, or babies. It's a place where people usually marry young and stay married their whole lives, which seem to last longer than people who live in other places.

The city swimming pool opens the day after the last day of school and stays open until the day before school starts again. Kids, at least when I went there, were trusted to walk by themselves to the grocery store or the town's one restaurant for lunch if they didn't like what the cafeteria was serving. A row of picnic tables sat in front of the school where kids would congregate after lunch on warm days and wait for the bell to ring, beckoning them back to class. On cold days, they would instead congregate in the gym.

Nearly everyone in Willow Lake is related to each other somehow, either by blood or marriage, so news travels fast. I once heard someone say that if they got scolded by a teacher at noon, their mother would know before they got home from school to tell her at 3:30. It was probably true.

We weren't related to anyone in Willow Lake, though, which automatically exiled us somewhat from the rest. The fact that we had moved into what was believed to be a haunted house didn't help much, either. You compile that with my shyness, sadness about leaving Stefanie, and the fact that my two front teeth had grown in oversized and crooked and it's not hard to see how I wound up being picked on.

Hallie almost immediately found a friend in Ellen, a girl in her class. Carrie found a friend in a girl named Linda. My class was nice enough at first, but they weren't Stefanie. I felt at the time that my classmates treated me unfairly- that they didn't give me a chance. Looking back, I realize the problem was that I didn't give them one.

I made up my mind long before the first day of school that I hated Willow Lake and everybody that lived there. I didn't want to be there. I wanted Stefanie and Suzy and the old house. The sixth grade went horribly for me. I didn't like my classmates. My sixth grade teacher was, arguably, the toughest teacher in public school history worldwide. Their curriculum was different than that of Cavour, meaning some of what I was learning I already knew and knew well and other things I was nowhere near ready to learn. They were so much further advanced in math and science than I had been in my prior school, I didn't feel I could catch up. So I quit trying. In the English classes, they were further behind and I was bored with the subject matter, so I didn't bother with that, either.

Topping it all off, my mother had gone to work for a potato plant, meaning she wasn't home when I got off the bus- which was something I wasn't used to. My grades suffered greatly.

By the seventh grade, there was another new girl. Her name was Kelly. The other kids picked on Kelly, too, because she was quite arrogant and tried desperately to be the "bad girl" in class. She eventually picked up on their teasing me and, unfortunately, believed that by teasing me she could make them like her. Instead, she just made life harder on me and annoyed everybody else. It eventually got to the point that the others stopped teasing me because Kelly had made it uncool. Very few could stand her, but, somehow, she thought everyone was jealous of her.

There were moments when Kelly would be nice, but for the most part those times were only when she wanted something. Usually, she needed someone to lie for her. She'd compliment someone on their shoes, then immediately ask a favor. If you did her the favor, she'd leave you alone for the rest of the day. If you didn't do the favor, she'd tell you how ugly your shoes were.

I actually felt sorry for her. What she told me of her home life and the relationship she had with her mother was not healthy. She didn't seem to have anyone she could turn to, and I always felt that maybe that's what was behind her putting walls up. If she expected everyone to dislike her, and she gave them reason to dislike her, they couldn't disappoint her. So I tried to like her, but it got increasingly difficult by the day.

Sometimes, outside of school, she'd call me and talk to me on the phone like we were friends. Then, the next morning at school, she'd call me a name or make fun of my walk or my teeth. When I got braces, she made fun of those. She would try to get boys to ask me out on dates, thinking it was funny. When they refused to play along with her, she'd tease me and the boy both, claiming we liked each other.

She and I were also on the Oral Interpretation team together. I joined Oral Interpretation because it was something I thoroughly enjoyed. All three of my mother's daughters loved Oral Interpretation. We loved to act. We loved to read. We loved literature of all kinds.

Kelly loved getting out of school to go flirt with boys, which is what she saw Oral Interpretation as an excuse to do. She was, actually, not bad at the competition. She got many high awards. I agreed to duet with her, and she embarrassed me at nearly every meet by trying to "hook me up" with boys from other schools. That was the only Oral Interpretation season I was happy to see come to a close.

Nearing the end of my eighth grade year, Sparky was killed. He was hit by a car- the sixth or seventh time in his life- only he didn't make it through this one. I was sad about his passing, and on the last day of the eighth grade, I was too upset to deal with Kelly and her antics.

We were in Mr. Meyer's science class, turning in our books, when she started for the day. She was making fun of my posture. I have always had pretty good posture, and for some reason it annoyed Kelly. She was sitting, straight-backed in her chair.

"Hey everyone! Look! I'm Jenny Thomas!" She screeched, desperate for attention. Every time she spoke, at least three people in the room, teachers included, would cringe. I believe most if not all of us would have rather rubbed salt in an open wound than listen to her on any given day of the week.

When nobody laughed, she said it louder. When still nobody laughed, she started making woodchuck noises. Still nobody laughed.

But I was getting angry. She'd picked the wrong day. Not only was I just upset enough over Sparky to get really upset, but it was the last day of school for the year. What could they do? Suspend me?

Today was the day. All this Kelly torment was about to end, once and for all.

As we walked out of the room, Kelly walked ahead of me, holding her back as straight as she could. "I'm Jenny Thomas! I'm Jenny Thomas!" she called out to a group of seventh graders. The eighth graders hadn't been impressed. I guess she was hoping a younger crowd would be more appreciative of her witticism.

Kelly was short, though. No taller than five-foot-three, maybe. In good shoes. My sisters were both bigger than me and I had taken them down on numerous occasions. Before I knew what I was doing, I had a handful of Kelly's hair, pulling back on it.

"Say it again, Kelly," I heard myself say, just

before pushing her into the wall to the left of us. She turned around and grabbed my hair and soon we were wrestling in the hallway in front of Mr. Meyer's class.

A sophomore boy grabbed me and tried to pull me off Kelly, but was unsuccessful. I heard him tell one of his friends to get Mr. Kruse. As I continued fighting Kelly, I wondered why he'd sent for Mr. Kruse, whose classroom was upstairs. It didn't make sense at all, until I realized Mr. Kruse was actually in the cafeteria, only steps away. I saw Mr. Kruse grab for Kelly and felt someone else grabbing me. It was Mr. Ehrke, the choir and band instructor. I elbowed him in the stomach and immediately felt guilty for it. I loved Mr. Ehrke. He was and remains one of my favorite people. I didn't want to hurt him.

As the two teachers pulled us apart, we were forced to let go of each other's hair. That's when I first realized Kelly had scratch marks on her face. I didn't even remember scratching her. Unable to reach each other with our hands anymore, we started kicking at each other. I got her once in the stomach before we got pulled too far apart. I looked down to see her bleached blond hair, as well as my own hair, scattered all over the floor. There was so much of it, I wondered how either of us wasn't bald.

"Holy shit.." I heard one of the boys in our class say.

"Get to class!" Mr. Ehrke yelled over his shoulder. We were taken back into the science lab and sat in opposite corners while the teachers discussed with the principal what had happened. We were then each called into the principal's office separately. Kelly went first. Then, I got called back.

Surprisingly, though, I didn't get into any trouble. I was told that what I did was wrong, but I wasn't given detention. My parents weren't called. The principal actually asked if I was okay.

"I'm fine," I said, "I'm sorry. I just got mad."

He smiled at me and, I think, winked. "It's alright," he said, "I know."

For the rest of the day, nobody at school mentioned it. To me, anyway. Hallie got some comments about it from several teachers. One of which stating to her that I had "finally given it to Kelly." In a bigger school, they might have been fired for saying such a thing.

But this was Willow Lake. And small towns are different.

And, strangely, by the end of that day, I found myself loving the little town.

"Unable are the loved to die, for love is immortality."

-Antoine De Saint-Exupery

The summer after what my mother would later reference as "the Kellacking," Mama took us to see Grandma Hallie in Chattanooga for what would be the last time.

Grandma was dying. Her heart was failing her. She had been taken from her house a couple years prior and moved into an apartment where she could better care for herself. Soon, though, even the apartment became more than she could handle, and she was moved to a nursing home.

We drove to Chattanooga from South Dakota, just like we had all the other times we'd been to visit. When we arrived in Chattanooga, Mama went immediately to the her mother's side. She couldn't wait another minute to see Grandma. She knew, and we knew, that this would be the last time.

Grandma looked so small. When we walked into

her room, she was curled up in her bed asleep. From the back, had it not been for her white hair, she could have almost been mistaken for a child. She was so frail, snuggled up beneath her blankets, looking out the window. When she heard us walk in, though, she sat straight up in her bed and smiled. It was in her smile that we could still recognize her. But not really anywhere else.

We had heard she was sick, but my sisters nor I had prepared ourselves for how Grandma was going to look.

She told us about her nurses and the lady she shared a room with and how much she hated her physical therapy. She complimented us on how pretty we were, and how tall we were getting. She asked us if Mama had been behaving herself.

Hearing her talk, you would have thought she was as healthy as she had been the summer she helped us make the quilt. But the truth was written all over her. She wasn't healthy at all, and never would be again.

I kept looking at Mama. It killed her to see Grandma. I knew it did. It had to.

Grandma knew it was the last time, too. She kept squeezing Mama's hand and talked as if there had never been a thousand miles between them. It was as if Mama lived just across the hall and they had seen each other yesterday and would see each other tomorrow and every day from now on and there was nothing to worry about.

"You're staying at my apartment, aren't you?"

Grandma asked Mama.

"Yes, Mother," Mama answered, "That's okay, isn't it?"

Grandma grinned, "Of course it's okay," she said, "I've got some boxes in my closet," she started to explain, before Mama cut her off.

"The girls won't mess with anything in your closet, will you girls?" Mama asked, assuming Grandma was worried about her things.

Grandma gave Mama one of her looks. "Don't tell them what they can or can't look at!" she scolded- as if Mama were ten years old again, "That's what I was about to say. They can look through them if they want. There's pictures of you in there that they might want to see. Don't talk for me, Margaret, I'm grown."

Mama just laughed her apology.

Of course, we couldn't wait to get back to Grandma's apartment and prowl through the boxes. But we didn't say that. We waited, patiently, for Mama to decide it was time to go for the day. When we got back to Grandma's, we took our baths and then Mama let us get one box at a time down to look in it.

They were filled with pictures of my Mama and her brothers and her sisters. Some of us. She had a couple of my mother's report cards from school stashed away, where teachers had written notes about Mama not being a very good listener, and how, sometimes, she was mouthy. They nearly mirrored the notes on Carrie's school reports, which led to great jubilation by Carrie who had not long ago been scolded by Mama for not behaving for her teacher.

Then, there was Grandma's divorce papers. She'd been divorced in her early twenties, taking from the marriage little more than what she wore and one daughter. In the papers, she had stated she wanted no help from the father- just to be left alone. Grandma was as tough as Mama.

Looking through the pictures, and the papers, and the report cards it became clear to all of us why Grandma had mentioned the boxes. With every photograph and every page, we learned more about her and Mama. She had found a way to answer all the questions we'd never thought to ask before, and would never get the chance to ask again. She had letters from us and our other cousins that we had long forgotten about. She'd kept everything.

We stayed for several days in Chattanooga. Mama spent every minute she could with Grandma and, on the way home, we stopped at Edgewood Cemetery in Dickson so Mama could show us where her Daddy was buried and where Grandma would be buried.

Alice was also there. She had died two years prior. Her big heart finally gave out.

Mama stood on the ground next to the grave tjat was to become her mother's and told us about the little Edgewood church and how much she'd loved living near there as a child. We stood in that cemetery and she laughed and told us about Ruskin Cave and the hijinks she and her cousins used to get into

144

on Yellow Creek until, finally, she decided it was time to leave.

It was over a thousand miles back home, and I think she cried the whole way.

We were only home two weeks when Mama got the phone call at work. We were at home, as it was summer break. Mama came in from work early, sobbing.

"Grandma died," she said, "I already talked to Camille. We're leaving in the morning early to go back down there, but I need to go to Watertown and get something to wear for the funeral. You all get dressed and come with me."

She went to her bedroom and started pulling drawers out, looking for cleaner clothes to wear to the store, then walked into the bathroom to get a shower. She smelled like the plant.

We went upstairs and found clothes of our own and changed, just as she'd asked us to. I felt sorry for her. I couldn't imagine what it must feel like to lose a parent. When I came back downstairs, she was sitting on the edge of her bed. She'd finished showering and had gotten dressed, but her wet hair was dripping onto her lap as she held her face in her hands crying. I sat by her and put my hand on her back, not sure what to say. I've never been good at comforting people. I'm uncomfortable being comforted, so I always feel like I'm smothering others.

Finally, she pulled her hands from her face and looked at me.

"Are y'all ready?" She asked, "I'm going to have

to get you some McDonald's or something for supper, okay?"

"That's okay," I said, "Yea, we're ready."

"Okay," she sighed and stood up, "Let's get this over with."

We followed Mama to the car, and hardly a word was spoken the entire drive to Watertown. From our house outside Willow Lake to Watertown is about an hour. Maybe a little less. We didn't even listen to the radio. Mama said she was too nervous to listen to anything. Instead, the three of us listened to her cry and wished we could do something to make her feel better. But there was nothing we could do. There was nothing anyone could have done. The same was true while we were in the store. She found a dress she liked, and we all made a point of telling her how pretty she'd look in it, although none of us were sure it was appropriate.

As she pulled out of the mall parking lot, she didn't look. I wasn't paying attention, either, until I heard the eighteen-wheeler blowing its horn. I looked up and saw the driver's face. He was petrified. By the grace of God, we narrowly avoided being hit by him.

"I didn't mean to do that!" she yelled back, probably afraid we thought she'd gone crazy.

"We know, Mama," we said, "It's okay."

"Oh, God," she sobbed, "Don't tell Daddy. I'm sorry I wasn't paying attention."

Hallie looked at Mama from the passenger seat.

"Mama, I can drive," she offered.

"No, you can't," Mama declined, "It will only make me more nervous."

So nobody said anything more for several minutes. We just rode and watched the other cars go by. Throughout all the terrible things our family had been through together, Mama had never been so nervous she couldn't drive. She had driven us a million miles in our lifetime, for everything from cancer treatments in Nashville to South Dakota when, for whatever reason, she decided she couldn't stand Tennessee anymore. Every summer since the move, she'd driven us to Tennessee and back to visit our grandparents and other relatives. If there was one thing the woman could always do, it was operate a motor vehicle.

We were scared, not because we thought she'd kill us, but because she'd never been unable to drive before. The truck incident only showed us how hurt she was, and we'd never seen her that upset in our lives. Mama was strong her entire life, except that day. That day, she was fragile. Defeated.

It was she that would finally break the silence.

"It doesn't matter how old you are," she said, "I'm fifty-one years old. When you lose your mother, you feel like an orphan."

"We're sorry, Mama," Hallie said, reaching to pat Mama's leg.

"I'm sorry," Mama said, "For everything. For pulling out in front of that truck and because I know this is how you'll all feel someday."

I don't remember anymore about Grandma dying, except the next morning, early, Mama took us to Aunt Camille's and we spent the night with Catherine and Timmy and Uncle Tim. Daddy came home the following day and took us back to Willow Lake and the day Mama returned from Tennessee, he took us all out to eat.

After Grandma died, though, people in our family started finding dimes. It was mostly Mama and her sisters, but the rest of us would see them, too, sometimes.

It seemed whenever things weren't going our way, all we had to do was look to our feet, and a dime would be laying somewhere close by. A God wink, I suppose.

Or, maybe, a Grandma Hallie wink.

Daddy used to joke around that he didn't believe it. He'd look at Mama and say, "Y'all oughta save all those dimes. You'll be a wealthy bunch of sisters one of these days."

But I always believed Mama.

After all, Grandma was the one to tell us about God winks, so it only made sense she'd send a few of her own.

"The best substitute for experience is being sixteen."

–Raymond Duncan

When I returned to school the fall after my grandmother's death, I was in the ninth grade. A high-schooler. Only four short years stood between me and running away to California, where I intended to break out into the movie business and eventually marry a Backstreet Boy. Preferably Howie, although I wouldn't discriminate. I liked them all.

This was also the year that Ryan and Wade found their way into our lives.

Ryan and Wade's mother, Jane, was a friend of a friend of my mother and she needed a babysitter. My mother, having decided she no longer wished to work for the potato plant, agreed to baby-sit the boys after school until Jane could get off work at a nursing home in a nearby town, which meant the boys were ours from three-thirty every afternoon until, usually, around five or six.

I loved those boys. Ryan was the older of the two, and had been diagnosed with a form of autism as a toddler. Wade, although younger than Ryan, was the bigger of the two. He also had developmental disabilities, although I don't know that anybody was ever able to diagnose exactly what they were. He and Ryan were not the same in their habits or personalities, however.

Ryan was the sweeter of the two, but he didn't like a lot of contact with other people. He loved us, and he had ways of showing the people he loved how he felt without the usual hugging or touchy-feely silliness that most little kids are into. He loved sports- particularly baseball. He would watch ESPN and then rattle off different players' statistics at random, sometimes days after he had seen them. He also liked music, but tried to refrain from dancing. Occasionally, though, he would get carried away with himself and bust a move, which caused Wade enormous glee.

Sometimes, Ryan would try to say something, but there would be what I can only describe as a misfiring in his brain that would cause him to say something completely different than what he was thinking. Usually, when this would happen, he'd yell "Good Morning, Grandpa!" We all soon learned that when he spoke those words, he was trying desperately to say something much more important. To ease his nervousness, my mother would get all excited when he'd say it, and shout "Incoming!"

causing him to laugh. When he laughed, his nerves eased allowing him to say whatever he wanted.

Other than Jane, my mother was the only person I ever saw Ryan hug.

Wade was the mischievous one. And, secretly, my favorite.

He couldn't pronounce my mother's name. "Margaret" had too many syllables and consonants for him to wrap his mouth around. Instead, he called her "Ungret."

When Mama would have the boys, she'd make goulash a lot. They loved it, and it was fairly cheap and easy to make, so it only made sense. My sisters and I soon sickened of it, but the boys would ask for seconds and thirds. "Goulash" was also difficult for Wade to say. Because my mother made it for him so often, he changed the name to "Ungosh."

I don't know their father. I never met him. He and Jane divorced when Wade was a baby. I do know that he paid child support and came to take the boys on some weekends. Other than that, I cannot comment on him, because that's all I know. But the boys loved him. They talked about him frequently. Jane never did. She made a point of not discussing him in front of the boys, and I was rarely around her when the boys weren't somewhere close by.

Jane was, and I guess still is, a remarkable mother. She always seemed so tired, though. I guess she was. She worked every day, then came and got her boys and worked at home late into the night, just to get up early and start it all over again.

151

She kept a spotless house and her only companion besides the boys was her dog, a Basset Hound named Bud. She had a fenced in yard, and would let Wade out to play with Bud in the summer time. One summer, Wade set to work digging a hole in the front yard and eventually had the entire yard dug up. The hole was so deep that he would have to jump to get out of it and, on really hot days, he'd beg to go outside so he and Bud could lay in the hole and stare up at the sky. I guess it must have been cool down there, lying in that soil. And Wade loved to be dirty. He was the word "boy" personified.

Ryan didn't take to being dirty like Wade did. Ryan fussed over everything- his clothes, his hands, his hair, you name it. If it wasn't clean, or laying just right, or if there was the slightest wrinkle it would upset him.

Ryan wasn't as friendly with dogs as Wade was, either, and by this point, we had a new dog, Wassail. Wassail was yet another Christmas pup, although this time the gift was to Hallie. Wassail was a red miniature dachshund. I don't guess there's ever been a sweeter animal.

She loved to snuggle, and found a nice place on the back of the couch where she preferred to lay when nobody was paying attention to her. When the boys would dance in the living room, she'd get up and dance with them.

Even Patches, who hated all other animals, loved Wassail. Sometimes, when everyone had been gone, one of us would come home to find Patches and

Wassail together on the back of the couch. When Patches realized they had been spotted, though, she'd always get up and run away, growling at Wassail as if it was all her fault. The cat equivalent, I guess, of "I swear I thought she was eighteen."

Mama had gifted Wassail to Hallie for Christmas after Hallie had mentioned one day that she had never had a pet to call her own. Carrie and I had always had cats and dogs that we could call our own, but never her. She had been far too busy in her childhood to worry with pets, and now that she was older, I guess she felt she had missed out.

Wassail was a good fit for Hallie. I don't believe there has ever been another dog/human pairing that seemed more meant to be. Wassail was a lap dog. She was perfectly content to lay in someone's lap and snuggle. Hallie, being somewhat of a book-worm, was more than happy to lie around, snuggling Wassail for as long as Wassail would sit.

When Hallie left for college the summer after my Freshman year, it nearly killed Wassail. She slept every night for a month wrapped up in one of Hallie's old shirts. Then, she started her shameless bed-hopping. She'd spend part of the night with Carrie, then move to Hallie's empty bed for a while. If she got too terribly lonely, she might attempt to come sleep on my bed, as well. But that was always ultimately up to Patches, who had claimed by bed as her own long ago.

There's nothing quite as confusing as being woke up at three in the morning by two animals fighting at your feet. After a while, though, I got used to it and thought nothing more of their early morning fisticuffs than I did the sound of Carrie's radio playing in her room, which it did, all night every night.

I began to get along better with my classmates, as well. I participated in class debates, even getting in an occasional one-liner that would, sometimes, make some of my classmates laugh. I started realizing that I could be funny and likeable, and although some of my classmates were only nice to be polite, I started feeling like I was truly beginning to fit in. My grades improved- slowly. Although I still didn't like school. I managed to take most Fridays off, and the occasional Wednesday. Maybe a Monday here and there.

I didn't win any perfect attendance awards, that's for sure.

I did stay in Oral Interpretation, though, and it was at an Oral Interpretation meet that I met Aaron. Aaron was my first ever boyfriend.

He was in the same grade as me. And he had a nice car. And he was tall. And he came and picked me up every time he had the chance to go to a movie or to shoot pool or, once, he brought his brother and Hallie and I double dated with them to a karaoke bar where we met his parents, thus turning it into a triple date. I had a blast, but Hallie didn't. Apparently she and the brother weren't a real great pairing.

Aaron was everything a teenage boyfriend should be. He was always very respectful of me and nice, and never came to pick me up for a date that he didn't bring me something, be it chocolate or a rose or a CD he'd made especially for me.

But that was the problem. He was everything a teenage boyfriend SHOULD be. Not everything a teenage girl wants.

He was too nice for me, and, ignorantly, I mistook that for being dorky. So I broke up with him.

I don't think he and I would have lasted forever. We weren't really all that compatible. I do feel guilty about hurting him.

He had been on vacation with his parents in Mexico and had called me the night they got back to tell me he'd bought me something while he was away. I had been thinking about breaking up with him over the last few days, but wasn't sure how I would do it or when. When he told me he'd bought me something, I felt like I should go ahead and break up with him before he gave me the gift. I wouldn't have felt right accepting it.

He asked when he could come see me and bring me my present, and I realized that he lived at least twenty miles away. I didn't want to let him drive all the way to my house just to be dumped. So I did what I thought was reasonable and dumped him over the phone. I told him I didn't think we should go out anymore. I could hear in his voice that I hurt him. There are few things I've ever felt more guilty about. I'm not good at hurting people. It's not something I enjoy.

I would get mine later on, though, after I started dating a boy named Jesse. Jesse was older than me, and was heading off to college to play football. It was a brief summer romance that I foolishly thought would last forever. The week before he left for school, he let me know he had another girl waiting for him when he got there. I was crushed. But that's what I deserved, I guess, for wanting a bad boy.

My mother often said that teenage boys are the most vile of all God's creatures, and I'd never believed her until I became a teenage girl.

As the beginning of my senior year of high school drew closer, I found myself more interested in boys than I had ever been and it was then that I would meet a boy named Jason and the Thomas family would be transformed forever.

*"A man who carries a cat by the tail learns some-
thing he can learn in no other way."*

–Mark Twain

I first met Jason because of a mutual friend of ours
named Cassie.

Cassie lived between Willow Lake and Yale and
worked as a waitress in the Yale Café where Jason
was a cook. He was older than Cassie and I. She was
only sixteen and I seventeen. He was nineteen going
on twenty.

Cassie kept a picture of me in her purse and, one
night at work, Jason happened to look over and see
it. He must have liked the photograph, or else been
really desperate, because when she came to school
the following Monday she told me about him and
how he'd asked about me. It was then that she and I
decided I would go stay the night with her on that
Friday and she'd introduce us.

Our plan didn't go as we'd hoped, however,
when her father- older and wiser than the two of us-

didn't let us go to the café. We had to settle for talking to Jason on the phone. During that conversation, we told Jason about a school Christmas program that we had coming up and he told us he would be there.

I had never seen Jason in person before the night of the Christmas concert. He and I spoke on the phone a few times between the night at Cassie's and the night of the concert and she had described- to the best of her abilities- what he looked like. She told me he was tall and had dark hair. She neglected to tell me about his piercing, tattoos, and wallet chains.

In a crowd full of grandmothers, farmers, and teachers, Jason stuck out like a sore thumb. But I kind of liked that. He was different and in my seventeen year old brain I rationalized the situation down to, having already dated a nice guy and a jock- why not date a thug?

Jason and I tore up the road between Willow Lake and Yale for the next several months. At least once a week, we'd see each other. Usually, we'd spend time in Yale at his house. He lived with his mother, Marjean, and his step-father, Dallas. Both of whom also had tattoos and looked to be the textbook definition of "badass."

I quickly grew to love not only Jason, but his parents as well. Especially Marjean.

Marjean was quirky, but fun. The first time I went to their house, she spent the entire day teaching me how to bake. I think it was her way of testing me, and I think I passed.

Soon, Marjean started referring to me as her daughter-in-law, which got right under my mother's skin considering I was only seventeen at the time. But Marjean meant well. She loved me.

Marjean had three loves in her life: her family, her dogs, and her crafts. The woman was a talented seamstress and the only person I know that could sit down with a table full of scraps in front of her and manage to come out with something absolutely beautiful in the end. She loved to write poetry and draw.

Together, she and Dallas at that time had five dogs: Buffy- a Pekingese, Zipper- an American Cocker Spaniel, Dakota and Lakota- two husky/wolf mixes, and Montana- a Dalmatian. They were an unusual-and colorful- pack, for sure, but they were all very much loved. It's been my experience in the world that when a person has nothing else, they're the most kind to their animals. Jason and his family were no exception.

The community of Yale wasn't happy about the dogs, however. Soon after Jason and I started dating, Montana fell dead after a neighbor poisoned him. Then Dakota. And then there were three.

Marjean attempted to get the law involved when the dogs were poisoned, but being a small community, nobody offered any help. It broke all their hearts that they couldn't get justice for their dogs.

As hard as their little family looked on the outside, they were all soft-hearted. I saw it. Not many other people did, though.

My daddy didn't like me dating Jason at all. I can't blame him. Especially once he found out Jason had only recently been released from jail at the time he and I started dating. Jason had made an unwise decision with the help of two very unwise friends.

I didn't think he was as bad as my father had him pegged to be. In a way, I still don't think Jason is bad.

Jason actually showed me a different side of himself. He was kind, and funny, and easy to talk to. Despite popular belief that Jason only wanted to hold me back, I thought he was very supportive of me in everything I wanted to do in my life.

Jason also had a way of always putting me first in his life. Which eventually became the problem.

Jason lost his job because he was always leaving early or skipping his shifts to spend time with me. Then, as I inched closer to graduation and planning my own future, he didn't really have anything planned for his other than for the two of us to just be together. This scared me enough to tell him one night that he needed to get a job or get back in school or else I wasn't going to be with him anymore.

That scared him enough to move to Watertown, where I was planning to attend Vo Tech the following year, and search for a job. He moved in with friends and had a job within the first week. By the end of the second week, though, he broke up with me.

Along with a new town and a new job had come a new girl. I was absolutely devastated. I didn't really have many friends other than the friends Jason and I shared, and now-with things having gone sour between us- it seemed awkward to talk to any of them. Except Dan.

Dan was Jason's friend and - quite literally-partner in crime. He had always seemed like a nice person to me, though, and I valued his friendship. During the break up with Jason, Dan made himself available for me to talk to, which is a trick I should have seen right through. Being young and impressionable, though, I didn't, and it wasn't long until Dan had me exactly where he wanted me.

Shortly after graduation, I moved into an apartment in Watertown, expecting to go to work as a server at a restaurant. I was hired the week I paid the deposit on my apartment, then found out after moving that the guy that hired me was actually not qualified to do hiring, leaving me jobless. My parents agreed to help me out until I was able to get another job, though, so I settled into living on my own.

Having grown up in a close-knit family, I would get bored and lonesome in the apartment by myself. To alleviate my boredom, I would often go for walks at night, where Dan would often find me and join me. We'd spend hours together walking and talking. In those days, he was easy to talk to.

Soon, he started coming to my apartment to watch movies or we'd occupy ourselves with some other silly pursuit. I had an old footlocker full of photographs of my sisters and I as babies and other keepsakes that my mother had kept for me. When she had given it to me on moving day, she'd said "Don't forget to take that foot locker, it reeks of Cavour Elementary." She was right. But I loved how it smelled. Sometimes, on particularly lonely nights, I would open the footlocker up just so I could smell it and remember being little.

When Dan wasn't around, my only company was a hermit crab named Dave. I never thought I could actually love a crustacean as much as I loved that little guy. When the boredom finally got the better of him, causing him to throw himself off the kitchen counter to an early death, I was overtaken with grief and didn't go for my nightly walk for three days until Dan came to check on me and convinced me to come along with him to the rock quarries in Milbank swimming. He said the fresh air would do me good. I was afraid of the quarries. The water was too deep, and I had never learned how to swim well. He assured me he wouldn't let me drown, though, and the entire afternoon was spent in the water, him teaching me how to stay afloat. I was impressed with his patience in teaching me, and his thoughtfulness to have come to check on me, and the fact that I somehow trusted him enough to not let me sink to the bottom of the water and die. That day, our friendship had grown into more.

Shortly after our relationship turned romantic, Dan got news form his ex-girlfriend, Jamie, that she was pregnant. He assured me this was not possible and that their relationship had never been that intimate and that she was simply jealous and trying to get me to break up with him. I didn't believe him, but I wanted to, so I ignored better judgment and allowed him to move in with me. I had found work as a cashier at a truck stop. He was jobless.

Eventually, I realized that financially I was not able to cut back my hours after classes started if I was going to be supporting the both of us. So I withdrew my enrollment at the school so I could work full time. It seems my bad decisions were endless.

The further along Jamie got into her pregnancy, the more obvious it became that she was not lying about being pregnant at all. This is when Dan began to insist that the baby belonged to another man and that she was simply pointing the finger at him because she didn't know the other person's name, which didn't make any sense- especially if, as he said, they had never been involved sexually. But, I continued to ignore the obvious in hopes that if I pretended it wasn't true, it would somehow disappear from my life. Meanwhile, while I was working, he was seeing Jamie and telling her that he and I were no longer together and he wanted to be a father to the child, fueling a terrible fight between Jamie and I, causing us both unneeded stress.

Dan very much enjoyed the attention of having two girls fighting over him, but he had to look out for himself, as well. When the stress of the situation started getting the better of me, I started threatening to kick him out of my apartment.

He had to come up with a solution to the problem quickly or wind up homeless, and I was still gullible.

It wasn't long until I found myself a teenage bride expecting a baby of her own.

"The reputation of a thousand years is determined in the conduct of one hour."

–Japanese Proverb

As a person could pretty well guess, our marriage was not only short-lived, but difficult. We married for the wrong reasons. He married me to keep a roof over his head and avoid assuming the responsibility he owed Jamie. I married him because, somehow, I thought that by him marrying me I had won something. I had beaten Jamie. Poor Jamie, really, had done nothing to me. All the bickering and name-calling between she and I had only been the two of us repeating what others had said. What others had lied about. The problem with teenagers getting married and having babies is that, until a certain age, young people feel the need to keep unnecessary drama in their lives. The Jen-Dan-Jamie love triangle had resulted in enough gossip to keep the Watertown scandalmongers fed for nearly a full year until Jamie had a beautiful little girl and the DNA tests came back showing ninety-six percent certainty that Dan was, in fact, the father.

I wasn't as surprised by the news as I pretended to be. I felt like I needed to pretend I didn't know, even though I did, because if other people realized I knew, then I would look terribly selfish, which I guess I had been. Even before the DNA test results came back, I had started questioning Dan's commitment as a father. He wasn't a bad person. He just lacked maturity. We both lacked maturity.

Our marriage, which had gotten off to an abominable start anyway, was tested yet again when Dan was diagnosed with testicular cancer. He needed surgery to remove the tumor, which resulted in him being unable to work for several weeks. Which resulted in him becoming bored at home and feeling even more of a need to socialize.

He wanted to go out at every possible moment. I was far more content to stay at home and thumb through the big baby name book or make silly plans for our future together. Because I didn't want to go out as often as he did, he started lying to me about working late so he could socialize with other people alone.

At times, he would come home drunk and I'd pretend not to notice. I always brushed it off by telling myself he would change after the baby came. Once he held her in his arms, he would begin to think like I thought.

Hoping I could rush the process, I started asking him about the daughter he shared with Jamie. I asked him to see if we could keep her overnight some time. I told him that I wanted her to be a part of our life together. I think it was half to satisfy me and the other half purely curiosity that eventually prompted him to make the phone call to Jamie about visitation. Jamie, at first, agreed, but would often make excuses at the last minute to keep from leaving Madison, her daughter, with the two of us. This would infuriate Dan, but I understood. We had treated her badly. She was a young mother. A young single mother. Madison was her whole life. How could we expect her to hand her everything over to two people that had treated her like less than nothing since the day she told them she was pregnant?

So, one day, I gathered enough courage to talk to Jamie myself. I knew there were things we both needed to say. I knew we had both been lied to. I also knew that if my marriage stood even half a chance, it lied with Madison. Since marrying, I had started re-alizing some of the truths of the world around us, and he remained the same. I was sure the difference was that I, carrying a child, knew what it meant to be a parent while it was still unreal to him. If Madison became part of his life, he'd understand what I un-derstood, and things would get better.

Jamie was sweeter than she had to be that day. Certainly sweeter than most would have been.

I was surprised at how much class she had. She had been portrayed by Dan and his friends as any-thing but dignified to me, but that's all she was. A lesser person would have shut the door in my face, or cussed me out and told me what a horrible person I'd been. Instead, she was genuinely interested in me and my pregnancy and concerned about how I was doing. She never spoke the words, but I knew she knew that things with Dan weren't okay.

"Listen," she finally said, "I want you to know I don't hate you. I think we've both been lied to and I think you're probably a sweet girl," she paused for a minute, thinking about how to word what she would say next, "And if things with you and Dan don't work out and he ignores your baby, too, I don't think our babies deserve to lose each other because of it."

And with that one statement, we were bound by unwritten and unspoken agreement. No matter what happened, we would keep in contact. We didn't have to be friends. We didn't even have to like each other. But we were going to know where each other was because some day our children would want to know about each other. We didn't know when or how we would tell them our story. That was a bridge we would cross when we came to it.

We did know, though, that we would come to that bridge together, as unlikely allies in our greatest battle yet.

As I prepared to welcome my first daughter, my mother had big changes planned for her own life. She had been to see a doctor who had informed about a gastric bypass procedure in which he would reduce her stomach to the size of a grape, enabling her to lose weight.

Mama had been overweight for most of her life. She had tried dieting and several other unhealthy ventures throughout her life to lose the weight and been unable to. In fact, the only time she'd ever reached her target weight was before she had been diagnosed with a hyperactive thyroid. Once that problem was corrected, she gained all her weight back quickly, which she would later insist was the cause of the diabetes that her doctor had all but promised the gastric bypass would cure.

She was so excited when her insurance approved the surgery. She and I had gone shopping that day to buy a crib for the baby, and while we were in the store she could hardly contain herself. One of my teachers from Willow Lake was shopping in the same store we were that day, expecting a baby of her own. She'd smiled at me over a clothing rack and asked, "Jenny are you getting excited?"

Before I could answer, Mama grinned, "I am! This will be my first grandbaby. My stepchildren have babies, but this is the first one of mine to have one."

The teacher laughed and politely said, "That is something to be excited for!"

Mama nodded and then added on, "I'll tell you something else, too! I'm getting a gastric bypass. By this time next year, I'll be skinny and healthy and chasing my grandbaby around. I can't hardly stand the waiting."

When she went and had the surgery a few weeks

later, she had what the doctor referred to as "minor complications," but was sent home.

By the time Mama had the surgery, Dan had found work at a grocery store, stocking shelves at night. The baby, whom he had named Nevaeh upon us finding out she was a girl, kept me up most of the time, anyway kicking and rolling over. She was very active. Because I had a hard time sleeping anyway, I would sit up all night most nights and wait for Dan to get home from work at four in the morning and we would go to bed together.

Because I was awake all night, I would sleep away the mornings. On one particular morning, the phone seemed to ring more than usual, but I ignored the calls, assuming it was one of the many credit unions that, by that point, tormented us daily trying to collect on Dan's hospital bills that we couldn't afford to pay. Eventually Dan, who was also trying to sleep, nudged me to get up and answer the phone so that whoever it was would quit calling us. By the time I got to the phone, it had stopped ringing, so I checked the Caller ID and found several calls from my mother's house and two from the hospital. I knew, then, that something terrible had happened. When I glanced at the answering machine, it was flashing an alert for three messages.

I punched the play button and instantly heard Carrie's voice. She was sobbing.

"Jenny, something's wrong with Mama," she cried, "Pick up. I know you're home. Just pick up. She fell and I don't know what to do. She can't talk or anything," I listened as she cried into the phone for about ten more seconds, waiting for me to pick up. "Jenny!" she screamed, "PICK UP!"

There was another ten seconds of crying, then the sound of her hanging up. The machine beeped to alert me of the end of the first message. I punched play again to hear the second.

"Jenny Mama's on her way to the hospital," Carrie said, "Sylvia's with her. I think she's going to die. Just thought I'd call you. Please get up and go down there," more crying found its way through the speakers, "I'm waiting for Aunt Camille. She's on her way to get me. Just get up and go to the hospital, okay? Bye." She hung up again.

The third message was Sylvia, Mama's neighbor and good friend.

"Hello, Jenny," she said, "It's Sylvia. Your mom is at Prairie Lakes. They need you to come down here, honey. They have to airlift her to Sioux Falls heart hospital and they need someone to sign the paperwork. I'm not family and Carrie's too young and I'm not sure when your Aunt is going to be here so come as soon as you hear this okay? I love you. Bye."

I ran to the bedroom and started throwing on my clothes.

"Dan!" I yelled, "Mama's at the hospital. She had a heart attack and I've got to get down there to sign for them to fly her to Sioux Falls." I expected him to get up and drive me. I needed him to. My nerves had me shaking so frenziedly I could hardly get my jeans on.

Instead, he tossed me the keys and rolled back over.

I didn't have time to worry about him, though. I needed to get to the hospital and sign those papers before Mama died, if she hadn't already. How stupid could I be to have not answered the phone? After the second call, I should have gotten up. I shouldn't have waited for so many rings. I should have known there was something going on.

And how had I not heard Carrie leaving the messages? She yelled, for God's sake. How didn't I hear that?

If Mama died because I didn't make it to the hospital, I would never forgive myself.

When I got to the emergency room, the helicopter had already landed and was awaiting approval for take off. Because nobody had signed for Mama yet, they hadn't loaded her into it yet. I looked through the parking lot for Sylvia's truck and found it. I didn't see Aunt Camille's car, though. I had beaten her. I'd not checked the times on the messages, so whether Camille was there or not was my only gauge how long ago they'd been left. When I saw she wasn't there, I knew it had been within the last couple hours, and felt somewhat better.

As I walked into the Emergency Room, I heard Sylvia's voice call out, "That's her! That's the daughter." I didn't see her, though. She must have been behind the curtain with my mother.

A doctor stepped out in front of me.

"Are you Margaret's daughter?" he asked.

"Yes, sir. I'm Jennifer," I answered.

"We need to put her on that helicopter," he pointed out the door, "Can you sign for it?"

"Of course. Do you have a pen?"

He looked a little puzzled. "Don't you want to know anything about the flight?"

He asked it as if there might be en-route entertainment or a choice of chicken or prime rib.

"As long as it's going to get her somewhere where she can get help, then I'm all for it," I explained as I scribbled my name on the forms. Because of the messages, asking about her condition had been almost an afterthought. I've never been good in these situations, anyway, and knowing that she was doing badly seemed like enough information for me then. I didn't need to know details, just that it was a serious situation and she was in capable hands. Because I knew it seemed strange that I hadn't asked, though, I felt obligated. "What's wrong with her?" I finally said.

"Well, we think she's had a heart attack," the doctor explained.

I had, over the years, known of a few people that had only minor heart attacks and a few more that died instantly. Telling me it was a heart attack had only confused me more than I would have been had I not known anything at all.

"How bad is it?" I asked, suddenly wanting to know more.

The doctor looked at me, then down at my now

swollen belly. It was obvious that there was a baby coming soon, and knowing this seemed to make him more sorrowful, "Is there anyone with you that I can talk to?" he asked.

I knew this meant it was far worse than I had even imagined. People have a tendency to, for whatever reason, treat pregnant women like infants. Not only did it anger me that he didn't seem to feel I was able to handle the information about my mother, but it had also suddenly reminded me that as I stood in the hospital dealing with such a family crisis, my husband was asleep, blissfully oblivious to what was happening. I didn't know how I'd explain that one to the doctor, so I got defensive.

"No," I said, "I drove myself. I'm a big girl. Big enough to put my Mama on a helicopter, right?"

The doctor looked at me, nodded, and sighed. "Right," he answered, "I'm not going to lie to you. It's bad. I don't know how she made it here, let alone how she's going to make it to Sioux Falls."

I realized, suddenly, that I hadn't really wanted to know, after all. I wasn't sure what I was going to do from there. I didn't know if I was supposed to go with her on the helicopter or follow behind or if I was even supposed to go at all.

I was scheduled to work that afternoon and was sure my boss would let me take off under the circumstances, but not sure Dan and I could afford for me to. Rent was already late and he wasn't bringing his checks home. If I missed even one day, I'd be in trouble.

As I stood in the waiting room worrying, I heard two familiar voices coming up behind me. Carrie and Aunt Camille had arrived.

"What's going on?" Aunt Camille asked when she saw me.

"They're going to fly her to Sioux Falls. They think it was a heart attack," I said.

"Are they flying her right away?" Camille asked.

"Yes," I said, "They're getting her ready right now."

By that time, Sylvia had joined us in the waiting room. "Somebody's going to have to fly with her," she said, "and it can't be Jenny because she's pregnant."

"Could I do it?" Carrie asked. She was the baby. It was only natural that she'd want to stay with Mama, even if Mama couldn't do anything to comfort her.

Sylvia disappeared to go find the pilot and ask. Carrie was only fifteen. None of us were sure what the guidelines were to the hospital helicopter.

When Sylvia returned, the pilot was with her.

He walked by Sylvia's side until he got close enough to our group to speak privately. He pointed at Carrie and said, "I assume you're the one going up?"

Sylvia nodded from behind him.

"Yes," Carrie said, "Is that okay?"

"Absolutely. Just come with me," he nodded as he motioned for her to follow him. He stopped halfway to turn back and tip his hat at us. "We'll get her there, ladies. See you in Sioux Falls."

And with that, Carrie disappeared. Camille, Sylvia, and I waited and watched from the waiting room window for the helicopter to take off. I was nervous- half expecting the two of them to lecture me about not having answered the phone. But they didn't.

"Has anyone gotten a hold of Hallie?" Sylvia asked.

"I think she's at church," Camille said, "Carrie talked to her roommate. She said she would go get her."

"Someone better let her know they're moving Margaret so she won't drive all the way up here," Sylvia thought out loud. Hallie was at that time living and attending college in Brookings, South Dakota, about an hour north of Sioux Falls.

Camille nodded, and one of the two called back and spoke to Hallie's roommate, Mary, again. I don't remember which it was. I was watching the hospital staff load Mama onto the helicopter as Carrie stood to the side, waiting for her turn to climb up. I felt my own baby kick as I watched Mama's baby fight the wind from the propeller of the helicopter as she looked on and cried. I wanted nothing more at that moment than to run to her and tell her not to get on with Mama. My mind was racing. What if Mama died before they got her to Sioux Falls? What if Carrie watched it? She'd be all alone up there.

"I'm going to head down there," Aunt Camille said. "Jenny? Are you going to drive down?"

She was wondering, I think, if I needed a ride.

"She can ride with me," Sylvia said, "Then you don't have to come out of your way bringing her home later."

It made sense to me. "I'll ride with Sylvia. I just need to go home and call my boss."

"We'll call him on the way," Sylvia said.

It dawned on them both at the same time, I think, that Dan wasn't at the hospital.

"Where's Dan?" Camille asked. They both looked at me, awaiting the answer.

"He's at home. In bed." I answered, knowing how terrible it sounded.

They just looked at one another. As the helicopter took off, Sylvia grabbed my arm.

"Let's go," She said, "It's time to wake him up."

Several hours later, Sylvia, Dan, and I found ourselves in Sioux Falls. Hallie made it to the hospital before we did, and we beat the helicopter. Sylvia joked that they should have just put Mama back in her truck.

Because of Willow Lake being a rural community, the ambulance service- like the fire department- is made up of volunteer staff. All the EMTs would have been at home or in church on a Sunday, so by the time they got word that they were needed, changed clothes, and retrieved the Ambulance it would have probably been too late to save Mama. Instead, Sylvia had picked Mama up and sped her to Watertown in the passenger seat of her pick up. Sylvia had gotten Mama to the hospital before an ambulance could have and, now, she had beaten the helicopter.

I worried about why the helicopter was taking so long. Had something happened? Was there no longer any need to hurry?

I thought about Carrie all alone up there, and bowed my head to pray for her. About that time, the announcement came over the loud speaker that the helicopter was landing outside. Nurses and Emergency Room staff hustled together through the waiting room and outside to assist, leaving the waiting room in eerie silence.

I could hear Dan's rhythmic breathing in the seat next to mine. He'd fallen asleep, having barely spoken ten words to me all day. He was mad that Sylvia had woke him up and made him come. He had made plans to work on a car with a friend of his, and those plans had now been ruined. He didn't understand.

Sylvia had woken him up and made him come along because she, understandably, thought I needed him there for support. I was pregnant and somehow that makes us delicate. What Sylvia didn't count on was how unsupportive Dan would be.

Hours were spent that day in Sioux Falls on nothing but silence and waiting. Waiting for news from the doctors. Waiting for Daddy to get there. He was only in Minnesota trucking. It wouldn't be long.

The only time the silence was ever broken for any length of time was when Carrie told us about the helicopter ride and how nice the people were that were working on Mama. That made us all feel a little better.

When news finally came, it was already dark outside. We were told that she had not suffered a heart attack at all, but a collapsed lung and that the suspected cause of the collapsed lung was MRSA, a hospital infection, that she probably acquired during her gastric bypass surgery.

She would need to stay at least a week or maybe even longer. Daddy had arrived by this time and sent the rest of us home.

Dan and I rode back to Watertown with Sylvia. Hardly anybody spoke the entire trip and when we got home, I ran immediately to the shower to wash the hospital smell off of me. Maybe it's because my senses had been heightened by pregnancy or maybe I had gone a little crazy from the hormones compiled with the stress of the day. Or, maybe, it was both. But I couldn't get the smell of the hospital to wash off of me. I shampooed my hair eight times that night. Finally, I ran out of hot water and had to get out, still smelling the hospital.

Dan was in the living room on the computer talking to one of his friends as I dried off in the bedroom. I yelled out the doorway, "If I never see another hospital again it will be too soon."

He yelled back, "Nevaeh's in trouble, then!"

I looked at the calendar. Six more weeks.

The following six weeks passed rather quickly.

Dan lost his job at the grocery and had gone to work for a dairy farmer who provided free housing for his employees. It was a lucky break for us with a new baby due any moment, and I started to believe our little family might make it. Until his temper came back.

Dan had an explosive, often violent, temper. He had been doing better and controlling his anger for several weeks until we started inching even closer to the baby's due date. He began staying out later and with people I didn't know. When he'd come in, he would be at least drunk if not worse and he would want me to wake up and argue with him. When he was inebriated, nothing brought him more pleasure than fighting with me. He would always be sorry the next morning, but never sorry enough to not pick a fight the next night.

Looking back, I now suspect he had some emotional trauma from the cancer, and was possibly suffering a hormonal imbalance as well that impaired his judgment. I hope that was the case, anyway.

Because I was having problems with early contractions and high blood pressure, my doctor scheduled me for an induction on October 7, 2003. By the time that date rolled around, mine and Dan's marriage had, veritably, already ended. We were living together because neither of us knew where to go or what to do next. We threatened and talked about divorce all the time, but felt stuck.

We were both excited the morning I went in to

have the baby, but he lost interest rather quickly. I think he expected the process would be quicker than it turned out being. We checked into the hospital at one o'clock, and I fully believe he expected to be holding a baby by three.

He went for a cigarette break around five, leaving Carrie, who had come to witness the birth, and I alone in the room. Soon, I found out my friend Becky had also arrived, making the only people in the delivery room us three girls, and we were only teenage girls to boot.

Dan called the room from his cell phone in the parking lot with an elaborate tale of a friend in need. He had no choice but to leave us there. We were to call him when it was getting close to time. I had pretty much figured something like that would happen, so I wasn't as bothered by it as I should have been.

I think it actually bothered the nursing staff worse than it bothered me. One of the nurses was named Meredith, which had actually been my first choice for the baby's name before Dan had talked me into Nevaeh. I kept looking at her nametag, wishing I'd never promised Dan otherwise.

"Where's your husband?" she smiled at me as she checked the baby's heartbeat on the fetal monitor.

"One of his friends needed him to come help with something," I explained, half-heartedly, knowing it was a lie.

She gave me a knowing nod and smiled as she

walked out of the room. Dan returned a couple hours later, with his "friend." Carrie and Becky had gone to get something to eat and I was alone in the room when they walked in. The friend wasn't a guy, as I had expected. It was a girl. A pretty red-head.

"Oh my god!" she screeched, "Danny should have told me you guys were having the baby, like, right now! I would have called somebody else. My car was stuck!"

I was angry, but I didn't want to be impolite. "It's okay," I said, "Did he get you unstuck?"

"Yea, I got her out," he grinned. She playfully slapped his arm. My heart pounded in my chest and I could feel my face getting hot. I wanted to scream at them and cry. It was one thing to leave me at the hospital alone and run to her. And another thing to bring her to the hospital with him. And yet another to stand there in front of me, while I'm in pain trying to give birth to his daughter and not only flirt with her, but allow her to flirt back. Nurse Meredith walked in behind them. As she took my blood pressure, Dan and the girl continued to tease each other back and forth. At one point, he had her in a half-headlock, tickling her ribs. I didn't even have to speak.

Nurse Meredith took the stethoscope out of her ears and raised her voice, "She has to go. Your wife is in a lot of pain and she's tired and you need to sit over here and help her through this."

The girl looked at Dan the same way I used to look at Dan. She was hoping and praying he'd say something to indicate that he had chosen her. It was written all over her face, just as it had been written on mine the day Jamie broke the news she was pregnant. But Dan didn't defend the girl. He looked at me, kindly, and asked, "Do you want her to?"

As crazy as it now seems, my heart broke for the girl. But the truth is that I didn't want her there. "He's off tomorrow," I smiled at her, "You can call him in the morning."

Dan reached out to hug the girl good night. The girl nodded at me, and gave Dan his hug and the way I looked at her, Nurse Meredith was looking at me.

The pain built for several more hours before the baby finally came. It's amazing how much pain a person can endure, and how quickly it washes away the second they see their new baby's face. The nurses had to clean her off and weigh her, and I cried. Literally sobbed because I didn't want to let her go. They gave her back to me when they were finished. She weighed exactly nine pounds and was twenty and one half inches long. She had a few tufts of dirty blonde hair and the bluest eyes I'd ever seen. She snuggled right into me immediately and fell asleep, and I knew then that all I'd ever wanted in life was that moment. I could lay there in that hospital bed and hold her until the end of forever, and I wanted to.

Becky and Carrie left first. Shortly after, Dan left, too. And it was just the baby and I in the room.

At around six in the morning, Nurse Meredith brought me some paperwork.

"You don't have to fill all this out right now," she said, "Just do it before you leave. It's your paperwork for the birth certificate." I reached out for the clipboard, which she handed to me. "Do you need a pen?" she asked. I looked around and didn't see one on my bedside table.

"Yes, please," I nodded.

"I'll be back in a minute," she winked and walked out of the room.

When she returned, she extended her hand, grasping the pen, towards me. When I tried to take the pen from her hand, though, she wouldn't let go. I looked into her face to see what was wrong.

She was giving me the look again. The one I'd given the redhead.

She leaned in close to quietly explain herself. "I need to tell you something," she said, never looking away from my eyes, " And I know it's not any of my business and it's not my job as your nurse to hand out advice. Don't take it as advice from a nurse, though. It's advice from a fellow mother. That boy isn't going to be around forever. He's barely here right now. Don't name her something you don't like because you promised him you would. He's promised you things, too, I'm sure and he's about to let you down on nearly all of it. Don't fall for that. You'll be raising her. Call her something that won't make you sick every time you hear it."

Without giving me a chance to talk back, she let go of her end of the pen and walked out of the room, shutting the door behind her. The baby was wrapped in a pink blanket next to me on the bed, her feet resting on my stomach. I looked at her, saying

"Nevaeh" in my head. I couldn't make the name fit.

So I started sifting through my memory for all the other names I'd considered, hoping to find a match. I decided naming a baby was a far bigger responsibility than I had counted on it being. I glanced down at the birth certificate forms as I thought back, and saw Nurse Meredith's name scribbled in the "Witness" blank. I felt my heart swell as I looked down at my daughter.

"Meredith," I whispered. I thought I saw her smile. She had her name.

I fell asleep that night with her head on my chest, whispering her name into her ear because I knew if I called her Meredith enough times, there was no way I would ever let Dan talk me out of my decision.

As I slept, I thought I felt my mother's hand brush the hair from my face, but by the time I opened my eyes, I only saw the back of Nurse Meredith leaving the room, filled-out forms in hand.

That was the end of her shift and I never saw her again. I think of her often, though, and wonder if she thinks of us.

"Your worst humiliation is only someone else's momentary entertainment."

- Karen Crockett

My marriage to Dan, not surprisingly, did not survive. I wound up back in Huron, having moved from Watertown shortly after Meredith's birth. Dan had moved to the town of Aberdeen, South Dakota, but frequently came to Huron to visit his mother and siblings.

Meredith and I shared a one bedroom apartment on Third street. It was an upstairs apartment in what had used to be a large house, but had been renovated as rental property many years ago. The apartment was, in all actuality, not suitable to have a baby in, but it was all I could afford. The foundation of the old house had crumbled away, leaving large cracks through all the walls. In the living room was a large stained glass window that in it's day had probably been beautiful, but now after years of wear and tear pieces of the glass were missing. The owner of the building had taped over the smaller holes and stuffed rags in the larger ones to keep the wind out.

The only heat source was an electric fireplace in the living room that only worked some of the time. Because I was on the upper floor, though, the heat from the downstairs apartments rose through the air ducts, which was the only thing that kept us from freezing that winter. The walls had once been beautifully papered with pink pastel roses on a white background, but old age or a prior tenant had half-stripped the paper off. Only some walls remained papers and the rest were yellow glue against plywood. The carpeting was old, as well, and unraveling in many places. All the furniture I had in the living room was a love seat and a television that only picked up three channels on a clear day and one if it was raining.

Off the living room was the smallest bathroom I've ever had the misfortune of peeing in. It was only a half step in the door before you were standing in front of the rust-stained sink, then you had to swing yourself to the left to sit on the toilet or sidestep right into the shower. There wasn't any room to move around in there, at all, so you had to dress and undress in the small hallway-like area outside the bathroom door, which sat directly across from the from the front door to the apartment. The front door knob only had to be rattled hard to come unlocked, so I learned to dress and undress at a rapid speed because I was paranoid about someone walking in on me. At night, when I didn't need the small hallway as a walk-through, I would use a chair from the kitchen table to secure the door shut.

The kitchen was the only halfway decent room in the house. It was small, with old cupboards and one large round sink. The old avocado colored refrigerator clashed against the golden cook stove, but they both worked and that was all I cared about. From the kitchen table, I could see out the kitchen window towards the lights of Dakota Avenue. From there, Huron seemed like a huge city. I used to like to sit at that table with a cup of coffee after I would get Meredith to sleep and look out that window and pretend I was somewhere else. Somewhere where she and I might have a fighting chance.

She slept in my bed. I had her crib set up, but that always seemed like she was too far away. Instead, I used the crib as a laundry hamper and put her between me and the wall at night. I'd barricade her onto the bed with pillows when I wasn't in there.

My bedroom was small and tucked away into the darkest corner of the already dark tenement. I had a double bed with springs poking through the mattress and one old dresser that held all my clothes and Meredith's.

Below my bedroom was an apartment that occupied a nosy old woman and her husband, who would frequently accost me at the mailbox with questions about things that were none of their business. They meant well. They were the type of busybodies that wanted to rescue those they felt less fortunate than themselves. Who better than the single teenage mother that lived upstairs?

But I didn't want their help. I wasn't comfortable taking anything they ever offered me. Sometimes, I would return home from work to find blankets or clothes sitting on my front doorstep and I knew they were the ones that left them there, so I would move the gifts back to their doorstep and leave them. Eventually, they stopped leaving me things, but I would get phone calls from church organizations asking if they could help me buy groceries or pay my phone bill and I would have to explain that I didn't want their help. Dan's favorite threat was that he would turn me into Child Services and tell them I couldn't care for my child. I knew enough to know that if he ever did, accepting financial help from strangers would only make a bad situation worse. My worst fear was that she would wind up in the foster care system, which is where he said he wanted her. He didn't want custody. He just didn't want me to have it.

Dan was as unpredictable as ever. He would go through phases of being a wonderful father, coming to see Meredith every chance he got and paying his child support regularly. Then, abruptly, he'd stop everything. There would be no child support. There would be no visits. Not even phone calls.

As his behavior became less and less predictable, his alcohol abuse became more and more apparent.

There would be times where I would see him around town, perfectly sober, and we would be able to speak civilly without fighting. There were other times where he would seek me out, asking mutual acquaintances where I was or he might just drive around aimlessly until he saw my car- all for the sole purpose of starting a fight.

I tried to avoid him at all costs, often refusing to go out in public unless I had to. I never knew when he was in town and became somewhat of an agora-phobic.

Of course, leaving was never completely avoidable. I had to work and I had to buy groceries. And, when he really wanted to, it was never hard for Dan to find me.

One night, I was working an evening shift at a local hotel, one of several jobs I had. I worked later shifts there, and it normally this worked out well because a friend of mine was available at that time to baby-sit.

When I got off work, I picked Meredith up and was on my way home when it occurred to me that we were out of diapers. I only had one left at home and I had to work in the morning. If I was going to get any, I had to do it right away.

So instead of going straight home, which my gut told me I needed to do, I went to the 24-hour grocery on the edge of town. It was the only place open at eleven-thirty on a week day.

I bundled Meredith in my jacket, trying not to wake her, and carried her inside with me. Once in-side, I sat her down in the cart. She was grumpy, of course. She thought I was taking her home to bed. I apologized to her for having her at the store so late, and made a bee-line for the baby aisle to get some diapers so I could get her home and to bed. I got the package of diapers and remembered we were also low on milk. I was at the store, anyway, it only made sense to pick up a gallon.

I should have waited on the milk. As I walked towards the dairy cooler, I had to pass the alcoholic beverage aisle where, of course, Dan and his buddies were shopping.

"Food stamps must be in.." I heard him comment to one of his friends. They had a good laugh at my expense and I hoped they would drop it. Instead, they started following me.

"It's pretty late to have the baby out, don't you think?" one of his friends asked. I didn't know the guy, which only made his comment even more loathsome, since it was purely to impress Dan.

"Yea," Dan added, "I thought you were a good Mommy."

I don't know why I have always felt it necessary to justify myself to him, but nevertheless, I tried. "She's low on diapers and milk and I have to work in the morning. It's just a quick trip."

"Who's watching her while you work tomorrow?" the elf-like female that accompanied them asked, "Got a new bed buddy?" She snuggled up to Dan's arm, obviously thinking it would hurt me.

"It certainly won't be YOUR new bed buddy," I answered, somewhat pleased with my response, but afraid of what they'd come back at me with.

"I don't like her wearing shit like that," Dan

continued, "hand-me-down shit. You've got on new pants. Why is she wearing something you got at a rummage sale?"

I noticed a young couple, obviously distracted by Dan's loud mouth, turn to stare. I felt my face getting flushed. I was humiliated. Call me anything, but don't call me a bad mother. "I needed new pants so I could work," I explained, "They have a dress code, and I didn't have anything that was decent to wear."

"Well now our daughter doesn't," Dan persisted, "So I don't know what you're working for." The couple was still staring. I was ashamed, and looked down at the floor, trying not to make eye contact with them, or Dan's friends, or Dan. Or Meredith. I couldn't face her. Part of me believed Dan was right.

When my eyes landed on the floor, I began watching my feet as I walked and pushed the cart.

"What are you going to do, cry?" He asked, "Cry your way out of it- just like you always do. Nobody here feels bad for you. You brought this all on yourself. Never should of ended it, Jen. Never should have.." I wanted so badly to turn around and scratch his eyes out, but I couldn't. I was weak. I kept walking.

"Dan, let's just leave her alone," the male friend suggested. I sensed guilt in his voice.

"Why should we leave her alone?" Dan slurred, "It's fun to fuck with her."

Just as he said it, my eyes, still following the dirty tile floor, landed on a dime and without realizing I was stopping, I did and heard words I did not feel forming escape my lips. "Go to Hell."

The group grew silent, but only for a few seconds. I turned and faced Dan. I made eye contact. For the first time in months, I didn't lower my head to him. I stood- inches shorter than him- with my chin up, staring him in the eye. I waited for him to respond.

"What did you say?" He finally asked.

"You heard me," I spit back, "Go to Hell." I wasn't afraid of him then. Not there in the store. Enough people were watching.

Before he had a chance to respond, I heard more words spilling out of me.

"I'm here in a grocery store after working a ten-hour shift trying to buy diapers and milk for your daughter, and I can't even do that in peace without worrying about you being here, waiting to piss on me. I've lived this way for months. I'm afraid to leave my apartment when I know you're in town because I have come to expect this from you and from every day of my life. I'm tired of it. I work my ass off to take care of her. I worked my ass off to take care of you. I was a GOOD wife to you, Dan. You had everything you owned in a duffle bag when you came to live with me. Everything you've got you owe to me, including your daughter. I quit school to take care of you and her. I do the best I can with what I've got. She's clothed. They may not be the cutest clothes in the world, but she's warm and she's clean and that's all any decent parent would care about. She's fed. She's loved. She's never been late for an immunization. She goes to the doctor when she's sick. And I deal with her hurt feelings when you show up to visit her and leave twenty minutes later because you're bored with being a dad. She waits two weeks at a time to see you and all you can give her is twenty minutes? Why?"

The elf stood, mouth agape, in disbelief. I don't think she was in disbelief because she had learned anything new about Dan as much as she was in disbelief that I would call him out. The couple was still watching, too. The girl was doing her best not to laugh. The boy gave me a thumbs up. I continued..

"I'll tell you why. Because your visits are in the afternoon, and it's too much to ask of you to stay sober past morning. That's why you're here in a grocery store with a couple teenagers drunk off your ass on a Tuesday night trying to pick a fight with a woman. Who's buying? One of them? Even when you work, you never have any money past the weekend. It all goes to beer and cigarettes. Hell, you'll borrow money from your mother for beer and cigarettes- what else? Maybe a little pot, too? But don't ask you to come up with diaper or milk money. That's an unrealistic request. How dare anyone expect you to take care of anyone but yourself- even if it is a life you helped create? Then you have the audacity to bitch about her clothes? You don't like what she's wearing- BUY HER SOMETHING."

I couldn't go on. I was afraid I'd start sounding crazy, which I actually probably already had. I wanted to leave it on a high note. As I turned to walk away, I didn't hear their footsteps behind me. I did hear someone – probably half of the couple- clapping.

"Fear is a great teacher. It shows you what you still need to learn."

-Roberta Hollander

The little apartment on third street did not have a washer and dryer, nor was there a coin wash in the building. To do my laundry, I had to carry a basket at a time about a block down the road to a bar that had a Laundromat in the back room. Because it was a bar, and because I had Meredith, I always had to go right away when the doors unlocked at noon before the bar crowd started funneling in for the night.

Across the street from the bar was a well-known party house in town where many of the friends Dan and I had shared frequented throughout the day and night. Often, I would be fighting the stroller and the laundry basket down the road and I would see some of them on the front porch talking. There had been a time where they would have shouted a hello across the street or offered me a beer. They might even have run to assist me with the load I was carrying. Any more, though, they pretended not to know me.

The Laundromat, although close to home and in a small town, was not safe enough to leave laundry unattended, so I would often bring a book or magazine to occupy myself while I waited for my clothes to finish. I always had Meredith in tow, though, and sometimes she made reading impossible.

To appease her, I bought six or seven colorful rubber balls from a quarter machine at the grocery store that I would throw in with the laundry sometimes. She would watch the balls bounce around with the clothes inside the washer. Sometimes, one would ping the door and she'd let out a shriek. Mothers have to be tricky to get anything done, it seems.

I almost always had the Laundromat to myself since most people without washers and dryers of their own were now using a newer, larger facility on the other end of town. The appliances were bigger at the other place and there were arcade games to play while you waited. I preferred the smaller Laundromat. It was closer to my home, and I could usually avoid having to deal with other people.

One of my friends and I had worked out an arrangement for me to do their laundry in exchange for them keeping Meredith for thirty minutes a day so I could avoid paying her Day Care overtime costs. Because I would often have their laundry plus my own and Meredith's, I usually wound up spending several hours in the back room of that bar waiting on their two ancient washers and one even older dryer to finish the job, but I didn't mind. That was the one place that I knew nobody would come looking for me. Not Dan. Not any busybodies. Not even any of my friends. When I was in the Laundromat, I was left alone to think of ways to make Meredith's life better. It nearly killed me that she didn't have all the things other babies had, and I was afraid she never would.

One evening, I gathered my laundry and put Meredith in her stroller to make the trip to do my wash. As I pushed her across the street and into the back room of that little liquor store, a man who lived a few houses down came out his front door, basket of laundry in hand. Of course he was coming over to do his own laundry, and I thought nothing of it. It was a Laundromat, after all, and laundry is a common chore.

I breathed a sigh of relief that, on this day, I only had my own wash to do. My friend had gone home for the week. I walked into the Laundromat first and started unloading my basket into the faster washer of the two, hoping I could beat the other guy to the dryer. Once I got the clothes started, I sat in one of the chairs and pulled Meredith's stroller close to me. I opened a bag of animal crackers for her and pulled out a book of crossword puzzles from the diaper bag.

The man with the basket of laundry walked in as I was getting comfortable and began unloading his clothes into the empty washer.

"Hello," he said. I looked up and smiled at him.

He wasn't as old as he had seemed when I saw him from a distance. In fact, he looked younger than me. He was very short and skinny and in desperate need of a hair cut. His brown hair hung out of the bottom of a dirty John Deere cap and the flannel shirt he was wearing was at least two sizes too large for him.

"I'm Jeremiah," he said.

"I'm Jennifer," I answered politely as I thumbed through my crossword book, hoping he didn't intend to converse with me the entire time we were both sitting there.

"Jennifer," he repeated to himself, whispering. It was then that I realized he wasn't quite right. I figured he had some sort of developmental delay, although he seemed to be very high-functioning. I decided to ignore his whispering, assuming it was probably something neurological, and went back to my crossword.

"I won't hurt you," he said, "I just like to talk, okay, Jennifer?" He was sitting down now, on the opposite wall so he could face me.

"Okay, Jeremiah," I answered, not sure whether to run or laugh.

"What is your baby's name, Jennifer?" he asked. I began to realize he was going to use my name every time he spoke to me, which explained his need to remember it.

"Her name is Meredith," I said, "But we all call her Tootie."

"Tootie," he whispered to himself. I couldn't help but smile. He didn't seem threatening at all.

Just a boy that liked to talk. He actually reminded me a little of Ryan and I had time to kill, so I put my crossword away for another time.

"So how old are you, Jeremiah?" I asked, trying to make small talk.

His worried face transformed suddenly from worry and nervousness into glee. Someone was interested in what he had to say. "I'm eighteen!" he shouted, then cupped his hand over his mouth, embarrassed at the volume of his voice.

I felt sorry for him for being embarrassed, so I shrieked back, "I'm nineteen!"

He started laughing, then, and rocking back and forth in his chair. Then, in his excitement, he began to twitch. It became obvious to me that I had been correct earlier when I guessed he had some sort of neurological disorder. Once he got himself under control, he looked at me, sadly, like he felt he should explain.

"I have something wrong with me," he said.

"I think we all do," I answered.

"My friend Brian has something wrong with him, too," he said, "We live together but we don't have a stove. Someone brings us supper every day."

There were a couple places in town that did outpatient programs for people otherwise unable to care for themselves, so I didn't at all doubt his story. "That's awesome!" I said, "I wish someone would bring me supper every day!"

He laughed. "Yeah, it's pretty sweet," he chuckled. He looked away for a minute and, when his eyes met the window, leapt to his feet. "There he is now!" he yelled, "That's Brian!"

I turned to see another boy, shorter than Jeremiah, walking into the Laundromat. This one had his head shaved and, instead of a friendly face like Jeremiah's, his was pensive, almost sinister, looking. He walked fast, with giant steps, and kept his arms crossed in front of him as he found his way to the chair next to Jeremiah and sat down. He looked over at me, then away quickly. I realized he had trouble with eye contact.

Jeremiah motioned towards me. "This is Jennifer, Brian, and that's Tootie. They're washing clothes, too."

Brian didn't say anything. He didn't even look at us. He just nodded. "Did you get all the towels?" he asked.

Jeremiah thought hard for a minute, then answered, "I think I forgot one in the bathroom."

"That's okay," Brian said. His voice was very quiet and difficult to hear above the washers. "We have to be at our meeting at two."

I suddenly felt guilty about taking the faster washer and decided I needed to make it right for them. "If my clothes get done first, I'll just wait anyway so you guys can have the dryer first. I don't have to be anywhere," I said.

Jeremiah smiled and slid his foot across the floor towards mine, giving my shoe a light kick. "You're so nice!" he said, "But we have a dryer. Our washer is just broken."

I must say it was a relief to hear. I didn't actually want to spend all day at the Laundromat.

Jeremiah was still impressed with my manners. "Did you hear that, Brian?" he nudged, "She would have let us use the dryer first!"

"That's nice," Brian said, still looking out the window. I decided Brian's problems weren't like Jeremiah's. Jeremiah seemed to suffer from a below-average IQ while Brian almost seemed too smart for the world. He was in constant thought, and his thoughts were troublesome. It was written on his face.

Jeremiah wanted to get back to our small talk. "Where do you work, Jennifer?" he asked.

"I work a couple different jobs," I said, "Mostly I clean houses."

Surprisingly, Brian smirked. "We could use you at our place," he joked.

I laughed, too. "Yea, mine isn't that great," I said, "I spend all my time cleaning other people's and mine just sort of gets ignored."

Brian smirked again. He turned and looked at me for the first time since looking away. He was thinking again. "Sometimes," he started, then paused-unsure of how to finish his statement, "You wear a red shirt that ties in the back."

The hairs on the back of my neck stood at attention. I did own a shirt like that, but I didn't know where he would have seen it. I looked to Jeremiah, who was obviously as confused as I was. His brow was furrowed and his huge mouth gaped open. We both looked back at Brian at the same time.

Brian's face was starting to turn red. He was embarrassed about even mentioning it. "It looks very pretty on you," he said, "I've seen you come in here before."

"Thank you Brian," I said, trying not to act afraid, although it was somewhat creepy.

"You're welcome," he said.

My washer buzzed. It was done. Theirs would be done soon, too, and they'd be gone. I stood up and walked to my washer to move my clothes to the dryer and Brian stood up as well.

"I should just go," he said, "I didn't mean to scare anybody."

"You didn't scare me, Brian," I lied. I strangely felt sorry for him.

"I scare everyone," he said as he ran out the door and back towards his house. I turned to Jeremiah, unsure of what to say or do.

"It's okay," Jeremiah said, "He's a loon."

Within minutes, the other washer buzzed and Jeremiah left. This was the last time I ever saw him or Brian. It was also the last time I ever did my laundry at the liquor store.

When I went back to my apartment with Meredith and my finished laundry and shut the door behind me, the lock didn't work, and a minute or two later the door swung back open from the breeze of one of the lower apartments fanning their door. I stuck my chair under the doorknob and wondered if Brian knew where I lived, since he knew where I did laundry and what some of my wardrobe looked like. For the first time, the little apartment on third street didn't feel safe to me and I knew that, somehow, I needed to figure out a way to afford somewhere better for Meredith and me to live.

"Love crowds out fear."

-Jody Strimling-Muchow

I was scheduled to clean a lake house at Lake Byron the next day, but the owner called me that morning and rescheduled me for the next week when they had unexpected out-of-town guests arrive. This left me with the day off.

Upon waking up, I remembered the incident at the Laundromat the day before and wondered if my tax return had arrived. I had already filed and was expecting the money to be direct deposited any day now. Once I got the money, I would be able to afford the deposit on a new apartment, granted I could find one cheap enough to afford year round. I decided to get Meredith up and dressed and we would go to the grocery store and I'd stop to check my account balance at the ATM on the way.

By a stroke of dumb luck, the money was in there.

I picked up a newspaper on my way home from

the store so I could look through the classified ads for a new place to live and found another one-bedroom apartment listed for only fifty dollars more a month than the one I was living in. The ad made a point of it being small, but I decided as long as the door would lock, it would be worth the extra money, regardless of how much smaller it might be than the apartment I was currently living in.

I called the number, and the gentleman on the other end seemed thrilled to have already had a call.

"I actually haven't even been over to clean it, yet," he said, "but If you'll forgive whatever mess we find I can show it to you right now."

I told him that was fine and immediately carried Meredith back down the stairs and to my car to go see the apartment, which was in yet another renovated house.

When I pulled up outside the building, I could already tell it was going to be nicer than the one I lived in. The yard was neatly mowed, there was a fresh coat of paint on the house, and- from what I could tell- no rags stuffed in the windows. The landlord was waiting outside when I got there.

"Is that your baby?" he asked. I had Meredith laying over my shoulder. She smiled at him.

"Yes," I said, worried that having a baby in the apartment might not be something he'd agree to, "But it's just me and her, and I work all the time so she spends most of the time with the babysitter and she's real quiet. She only cries when something's wrong and she stops right away, usually."

Before I could finish speaking, he put his hand up to shush me. "My mama raised me in a hotel room," he grinned, "And, actually, there's a great big closet up there that you could fit a crib into as a nursery, if you wanted."

He motioned for me to follow him into a side door that I immediately realized was a private entrance. I wouldn't have to walk past nosy neighbors anymore. There was fresh paint and new carpeting all the way up the stairs which led into a small hallway. To the left was a large bedroom with the biggest walk-in-closet I've ever seen. And the closet had a window. I could put her crib in there, if I wanted. Straight ahead was a large bathroom with a claw-foot tub and to the right was a large living room with a bay window. Off of the living room was a very small kitchen, but I could make do.

The apartment was perfect for Meredith and me. I had expected it to be smaller than the one on third street judging from the wording of the ad, but it was at least half again bigger. It was also closer to my work and only a few blocks from Meredith's baby-sitter.

The doors locked, the heat worked, and all utilities except water were furnished. I did the math in my head as I stood in the living room and slowly began to realize that, after all the math, I wouldn't be paying any more than I already was.

"They actually left it pretty clean," the landlord thought out loud, "If you wanted it, I could probably let you move in this weekend."

"I want it," I said, "I have the money for it right now if you want."

"Well, alright then," he grinned, "This is the quickest I've ever rented a place out!" He was laughing as he pulled out his wallet to write me a receipt.

"It's the quickest I've ever rented one," I laughed back.

When I left, I had the keys in my hand and an agreement to move in on the weekend. In order to move, though, I needed help. Luckily, I knew someone willing.

Robert was a good friend of mine, but at first I felt more for him as a buddy or an older brother than I did in a romantic sense. He was fun to hang out with.

He wasn't originally from Huron, either, and was also sort of an outcast. He had lived in Aberdeen the past several years with his ex-girlfriend, but the relationship ended badly and he had left Aberdeen for Huron, where he went to work with his stepfather. He spent most of his free time, until he met me, at his mother, Evonne's, house helping her with Erin, his little sister.

Erin was eighteen at the time, and had begun having developmental disabilities at around the age of three following a seizure. Her disorder has never received an official diagnosis, other than one doctor explaining that she would forever have the mentality of a two year old child.

Sometimes, when I had the day off, I'd go to Evonne's house and wait with Robert for Erin to get home from school. He loved to be there when she got home, because she was always so excited to see him.

The day Meredith first met Erin, we had been sitting at Evonne's dining room table much of the afternoon talking when we saw the van from Erin's school pull up in front of the house. Evonne pointed out the front window.

"Robert! Go help your sister in," she said.

Robert got up and went to the front door and waited for Erin to hobble her way to the front steps. I could hear her from the table.

"I need a Bobby! I need a Bobby!"

"Yea, Yea, Yea," he rolled his eyes, "I'm right here. Come in. There's a baby in here."

Meredith laid on a blanket on the floor-her big blue eyes watching Robert's every step. She heard Erin's voice, and it was interesting to her. She wanted to know who it was coming from.

Erin squealed when she came through the door. She tried to run, but that resulted in a wobbly stomp. "I need a bee! I need a bee!" she shouted as she reached for Meredith on the blanket. Meredith now became frightened and started to cry.

Evonne laughed. "She won't hurt her," she said, "She just loves babies so much. That's what she's saying. 'I need a baby.'"

"Yea, yea," Robert rolled his eyes again, "Don't we all need a baby?"

Erin reached over and started patting Robert's rounded belly. "Bobby have a baby. Bobby have a baby." She squealed in laughter at her own silliness.

"That's not a baby!" Evonne laughed. "What is it, though?"

Erin smiled and looked at me. "Beer," she laughed.

Robert rolled his eyes a third time. "Erin, why are you so mean to me?" he asked, pretending to pout. His dirty blond hair needed cut and hung out from underneath his orange cap. He also needed a good shave and when he fake-frowned, trying to hold his laughter in, his hazel eyes sparkled under the light. His scruffy look compiled with the sweetness that was him teasing his sister made me realize, for the first time, how cute he was.

I had actually come over on that day because Evonne and Robert were going to baby-sit Meredith for me. Her usual babysitter was sick and I was working a night shift at the hotel. At around the time Erin came in, it was time for me to go. I kissed Meredith good bye and handed her off to Robert, who had cancelled his own afternoon plans to help his mother with Erin and Meredith both.

As I headed into work, I thought about how silly it was to have a crush on Robert. I didn't have time for a boyfriend and boys had only ever caused me trouble in the past, anyway. When I got to work, though, my favorite co-worker was already there, having switched shifts with the person I was supposed to work with. I was excited to see her because on nights we worked together the shift always went much faster. Mostly because we spent most of the time gossiping about other employees and people we know around town. Her name was Jill and she'd never met Robert, so when she started gushing about a boy from her church group, I felt comfortable enough to gush a little bit about Robert, too.

"I never realized until tonight how cute he is," I said.

"Oh," she joked, "then he must be really hot."

"Shut up," I laughed, "He is. But it's not like Ryan Reynolds hot or anything. He's cute. Like you just want to pick him up and squeeze him. Like a hamster."

"So," she said, "he looks like a hamster?"

"Well no," I said, "He's hot." I realized then how stupid I sounded.

"So you're sexually attracted to hamsters?" she asked, as seriously as possible. Around that time, we looked up to see one of our regular businessmen in the hotel lobby buying himself a soda. We often referred to him as Al, because he reminded us of the character Al from the nineties sitcom Home Improvement. He had heard us. He was laughing to himself and shaking his head.

"It happens all the time," Jill shouted towards him, "Don't you watch The Learning Channel?"

He winked back over at us. "Glad you girls are having a good night," he said as he stepped into the elevator. The door dinged shut.

"Talk about sexy hamsters," I joked, causing Jill

to nearly drown in her diet Pepsi.

"He probably knows you like him anyway," she said, "you guys spend so much time together I'm surprised you aren't dating yet."

"I don't think he likes me that way," I said.

Jill looked at me for a minute, then bopped my forehead with her hand. "He cancelled all his plans tonight to baby sit for you," she said, "He likes you."

I hadn't yet considered the possibility that he liked me as more than a friend. There had been a couple times where he'd offered to buy me dinner and once he had paid for Meredith's milk in a gas station because he didn't want me to have to walk back out to my car when I realized I'd forgotten my purse. When I tried to pay him back later on, he wouldn't take it. I thought he was trying to be charitable, which had actually caused me to not talk to him for a few days because I hated being treated like charity. Eventually, he called me and asked me if I was mad at him, and I realized I wasn't, so we began talking again. I was glad because he was a good friend to me and I enjoyed the company.

I thought about him all night at the hotel, and when I went to pick Meredith up, he was waiting in his mother's living room. He was in her old blue recliner, with one leg up on the foot rest. The other sat flat on the floor. Evonne was busy trying to get Erin to bed, and Meredith had fallen asleep with her head on Robert's chest, a half empty bottle sat on the table beside them.

As I came in the front door, I was careful not to

make too much noise. I knew if Erin figured out I was there, she'd never stay laying down, and I didn't want to wake Meredith up yet, either.

As I slowly crept across the living room to the couch beside Robert and Meredith, I whispered, "How long has she been asleep?"

"Not long," he winked, "Did you know she says 'Mama' already?"

I didn't know. I was surprised. "Really?" I asked, "Are you sure?"

He grinned and nodded, "She was crying for you and kept saying Mamamamama," He leaned forward so he could cradle her in his arms to put her in the car seat for me. As her head left his chest, he kissed her forehead.

She stretched, yawned, smiled and went back to sleep. He stood up and bounced her in his arms while he waited for me to get the straps on her carrier moved so he could lay her back down.

"She just ate a little bit ago," he whispered, "She shouldn't be hungry for a while." I noticed a dried spot of spit-up on his black t-shirt.

"Ick," I said, "She gotcha."

He was confused at first, but noticed then what I was referring to. "Twice," he smiled, moving the blanket from his other shoulder to show me another spot.

I felt silly. Meredith was only five months old. Yet, there I was, wondering if Jill had been right about the way Robert felt about me. I was only nineteen then. Crushes and flirting wouldn't have been abnormal for a girl my age. But I had Meredith to worry about, and wasn't sure if I would, or should, ever be involved in another romantic relationship again. And what of our friendship? If Robert and I did date, and it ended poorly, I'd lose my best friend.

Evonne walked into the dining room after finally getting Erin to sleep. She smiled at me through sleepy eyes and said, "It was so cute, Jen, Erin was getting jealous because Bobby was holding the baby so I took the baby and then Meredith was getting jealous because Erin had Bobby." Robert grinned and rolled his eyes.

"Erin's a tool, Mom," he laughed.

"Oh but Erin just loves her Bobby," she laughed. She put her hand on my shoulder, "Meredith was so good, though. She's a sweet baby. Do you need us again tomorrow?"

"No," I said, "I'm actually off tomorrow all day and night. I need to go to the Laundromat and then I'm going home to sleep."

Evonne laughed. "I know the feeling," she joked, "But why are you going to the Laundromat?"

"Because I have clothes to wash," I said, "My building doesn't have a coin wash."

"Well we have a washer and dryer. Why don't you bring your wash here and then you can watch Erin for me while I go run errands?"

It seemed reasonable enough, so I nodded agreement.

"Good," she said, "Then I don't have to bring her with me and you don't have to fan your panties around in public."

"Mother!" Robert yelped.

"What?" Evonne screeched back, "I'm not allowed to reference Jen's panties?"

Robert was blushing now, and shaking his head. "I'm going outside," he mumbled.

"No, not yet!" Evonne grabbed his arm, "I just got an idea."

We both stood and stared at Evonne, waiting for what she might say next. "Robert gets off at noon tomorrow and I'll be done running errands by then, why don't you guys go see a movie and I'll watch the baby? You guys deserve a break."

I looked at Robert, wondering if he really wanted to go or not. He looked back at me, obviously wondering the same. "We could," I finally said, "If you're sure you don't mind."

"I don't mind at all! I love babies," she smiled at Meredith in the carrier.

Robert smiled. "See you when I get off then?"

"You bet," I smiled back. I started to pick up Meredith's carrier, but he picked it up first. "It's icy out there," he said, "I'll get her to the car."

He walked behind me outside and to my car where he strapped Meredith into the back seat for me. When she was in place, I thanked him for watching her and hugged his neck. He hugged me back and told me to drive careful. I thought, for just a second, about kissing him, but couldn't muster up the guts to do it. Instead, I just told him good night and drove home, kicking myself the entire way.

The next day, in the theater, I laid my head on Robert's shoulder and fell asleep. I missed the entire last half of the movie, but he didn't wake me up. He just let me lay there, only bothering me once to take my drink out of my hand and put it in the cup holder so I wouldn't spill it in his lap. When the movie was over, I was awakened by the sound of the people around me getting up to leave their seats. I was embarrassed that I'd fallen asleep.

"I'm sorry," I said, wiping my eyes.

He just smiled at me. "It's okay," he said, "I'm glad you got some rest."

"Thanks," I said, "Was the movie good?" I had to laugh at this question, since we'd come to see a movie that I wanted to see. He had wanted to see something entirely different, but I had argued him into my choice, instead. Then left him alone to watch it as I slept.

"It was alright," he laughed, "But I'm not going to lie. Some of the people watching it fell asleep."

"What losers!" I yelled back, "Who pays to see a movie and then sleeps through it, anyway? Dumbasses."

Robert laughed as we finally stood up from the theater seats. He turned to walk towards the aisle to leave, and reached behind his back for my hand. When he found it, I gave it a squeeze, not sure why. I guess just habit. He squeezed back. As we walked out of the theater, I felt comfortable enough to grab his arm. It was raining outside, and cold, and I guess I felt the closer I could get to him the better. Or maybe I just wanted to be close to him, and the weather had nothing to do with it. The latter is the most likely, I would assume.

We ran to my car together, and I let him take the drivers seat. I have a hard time seeing when it's dark or cloudy out, especially in the rain. I climbed into my car and slammed the door shut. I was soaked from the rain. My hair was wet and so was my sweatshirt. Robert wasn't much better off.

I was laughing about us being soaked when he leaned over and kissed my cheek. I turned and looked at him, somewhat surprised, and then he kissed my lips. I have to laugh about it now. It was almost too perfect. Like something out of a very poorly written teen movie. But it was real. And I was so happy it was.

"Our friends should be companions who inspire us, who help us rise to our best."

-Joseph B. Wirthlin

Soon, Robert and I were inseparable. Every minute he had away from work, and every minute I had away from work, we spent together.

For my twentieth birthday, Robert took me to see my mother in Sioux Falls. She had been released from the hospital for a short while, but was taken back when the infection returned. She was now being held in quarantine, and was not expected to live.

She had a tracheotomy and was unable to speak, but my Daddy had brought her a pen and a notebook that she would use to write notes to people. She wasn't expecting me when we got there. She had no idea it was my birthday. She never knew what day it was, anymore, and half the time she didn't know where she was. She was confused by her pain medication and would often ask my Daddy if he was mad at her because he didn't sleep in the bed with her anymore.

I was afraid she wouldn't recognize me when I got there. The last time I'd been up there, she hadn't. Robert carried Meredith for me up the elevator and down the long corridor into Mama's room. Her eyes lit up instantly when she saw me. She did know.

She tried to say my name, but wasn't able to and reached for her pen and paper to scribble. A few minutes later she turned the paper for me to see.

Have you colored your hair?

"No, Mama. I just let all the color from last time wash out."

Carrie and Hallie were there. They laughed.

Mama scribbled some more. *Are those new clothes?*

"No, Mama. I've had these clothes since high school."

Carrie and Hallie giggled some more. Mama scribbled again.

You've lost weight.

"Actually, I've gained weight."

Mama rolled her eyes while Hallie and Carrie laughed. She put pen to paper to scribble some more.

Pooey on you.

"Pooey on me?" I laughed as I read it. Carrie and Hallie laughed, too, and Carrie was unable to hold in her sarcastic remark.

"She got a nose job, Mama."

Mama grinned as she looked over at Carrie. She knew Carrie was kidding. She put a finger on her own nose, nodded, and mouthed, "That's it."

Robert had gone back to wait in the hallway for me. He didn't want to be in the room with Mama without her knowing who he was, and I had absent-mindedly forgotten to introduce him. Mama saw him, and motioned him in. When he walked in, she waved and smiled. He said hello and sat down with Hallie and Carrie, who had met him once before when I'd taken him to the farmhouse in Willow Lake. Mama motioned for me to get Meredith out of the carrier.

Because of Mama's infection, we had to be careful with Meredith around her, but the doctors had given us the okay to put Meredith on Mama's bed, as long as she didn't have a whole lot of skin to skin contact. Mama liked to sit up in the bed and put Meredith on her back between her knees so they could face each other. Then Meredith could put her feet against Mama's hands and kick, which for whatever funny reason Mama loved.

Meredith loved Mama. Even as sick as Mama was, and as scary as all the tubes and machines had to have been to a baby, Meredith would look up at Mama and her big blue eyes would just glitter as she laughed and clapped her little hands, pleased for the company.

When she'd clap, Mama would put her hands together, and clap along. Meredith's little fingers were fat and pink and her hands as white as the blanket she lay on, while Mama's hands were older and brown, with calluses and wrinkles covering any empty space they could find and her knuckles swollen, fingers bent from years of hard work and arthritis. But, both sets of hands belonging to people who could not at that moment speak words to one another, would clap entire secret conversations. The clapping and kicking along with the smiling and looking each other in the eye could go on for nearly an hour before one or both of them would get tired of the game at the same time. Then Meredith would give Mama one last look, with a little baby smirk added, as if to say, "Nice talk."

When Mama and Meredith had finished gossiping about me, or discussing the weather, or whatever it is they always did, Mama turned to Robert and smiled. That was her hello. The only one she knew to give.

He smiled a hello back and Mama scribbled on her paper, turning the page to show me.

I like him.

I smiled at her. "Me, too."

She took the paper back and wrote some more. *Head on home before it gets dark. I love you.*

And, after a hug, I left. She never remembered to tell me Happy Birthday, and I sort of forgot to expect it. I was just happy to be there with her and with Meredith and with Robert and my sisters. Surrounded by people that I knew loved me, when so often I was alone.

On the way back into Huron, we passed under the same overpass that my mother had driven us under all those years before, on the very first day I set foot in Huron, South Dakota. I thought about that trip, and how healthy she had been then. And I thought of all the years that followed, growing up with Mama, and all the plans I had made for being a grown up. I was going to be a veterinarian, but if that didn't pan out I thought I'd be an actress. It was a clinic or Hollywood for me. Nothing else.

I thought about Patches at home, left mostly alone these days due to Mama being in Sioux Falls and Daddy and my sisters always having to leave her there to be with Mama. I wondered if she ever felt as lonely as I did.

I wondered if Robert, or anybody else, understood why I was alone. If Mama and Daddy knew half of what went on in Huron with Dan and the apartment door that wouldn't lock or the creepy people at the Laundromat, they would both have heart attacks and die. I would lie to them, though, and pretend things were better than they were to keep them from worrying. I didn't want them to talk me into coming home. I needed to do this myself. And, being in Huron and worrying about my own problems in a way gave me an excuse to pardon myself from the problems back in Willow Lake with Mama being sick and the bank getting ready to foreclose on the farm. In a way, I was very selfish.

I loved them all, but I couldn't stand to see them struggle, and I couldn't stand them seeing me struggle, either. So, I rationalized that it was best for me to lie and pretend things were okay for everyone.

It wasn't long after my birthday that the bank did foreclose and Daddy, Hallie, and Carrie moved to

Sioux Falls to be closer to Mama. Not long after their move, Mama was released from the hospital and taken to her new home, which she loved, but not like she had loved the farmhouse.

She didn't have the quiet at night, or the privacy to go outside. Her chickens and cows were gone. So was Patches.

Patches had been given to a family friend to live out the rest of her days. I couldn't take her where I was living at the time. Pets weren't allowed, and I had Meredith to consider. Not long after Patches was taken by this friend, she disappeared and we all mourned for her, assuming she had passed away.

She was thirteen years old, which is a pretty long life for a cat, and it had been a happy one, filled with love and all the Alpo she could stomach. But we all hated that she'd died alone.

After all, it was winter time, and cold. And she had been thrust from her happy home into strange territory and a cold barn where it would have taken a miracle to have kept her alive.

An absolute miracle.

"Life is tough enough without having someone kick you from the inside."

–Rita Rudner

As things in Sioux Falls began getting back to normal for my family, things in Huron were improving as well.

My relationship with Robert was flourishing and I had discovered that Marjean was now living just around the corner from my new apartment. She and Dallas had decided to move into town and were buying a house literally a ten second walk from my doorstep. With Jason now living in Sioux Falls with his wife, Marjean and I were able to salvage a friendship from the ruins of my failed teenage love affair.

Not a day went by that Marjean and I didn't talk. I enjoyed having her back in my life. I could talk to her about all the little problems I had that I didn't feel comfortable discussing with my parents. When Robert was working and I needed someone to tag along to run errands, Marjean was always good to go.

She also knew Robert, and had known him since infancy. Robert didn't remember her, though. He remembered her ex husband, who had been friends with his dad. But not Marjean.

Marjean remembered Robert, though, and would tell me funny little stories about him behind his back while he was working. Things he'd done as a baby that she had witnessed, or stories about his dad. She loved Robert. And she loved me being with Robert. She encouraged our relationship, and that made me happy. I had grown to love Robert more than I had ever loved Dan, but I was afraid.

My judgment on these things had failed me before.

Robert, though, also seemed sure and had brought up the subject of marriage a couple times, but I always told him I wasn't ready to talk about it yet. I was only twenty, and already divorced once. I never wanted to get divorced again, and not getting married seemed to be the only logical answer to that dilemma.

Things changed in October, though, at around the time of Meredith's first birthday. I had become increasingly tired and lackadaisical around the house. Sometimes, I would sleep so sound that the alarm wouldn't get me up in the morning, and I would be late for work. Robert started noticing I was pale. When Marjean first suggested that I might be pregnant, I laughed at her. I had been on the birth control patch, and had been careful with it except for one week in the beginning of August when I had been on my off week and forgotten to put a new patch on when Monday rolled back around, so had taken an extra week for good measure. Besides, that was two months ago. If I'd been pregnant, surely I would be vomiting. I found out at seven weeks with Meredith and had already been throwing up for three.

I thought maybe I was anemic again, having suffered with anemia all my life. Robert, concerned about my health and not entirely convinced I wasn't pregnant, gave me the money to go see a doctor and get checked out. It was time to renew my prescription for birth control anyway, so I scheduled an appointment with my doctor and went in on a Thursday while Robert was at work. Marjean kept Meredith.

The nurse drew blood, and I waited for nearly an hour in the exam room before the doctor returned to give me my physical. When the doctor walked in, she asked what she could do for me.

"I need to talk to you about birth control," I stated.

She smirked, looking at the chart, and said "Honey judging from these lab results I'm going to guess you're about six weeks too late on that."

I felt my heart quit. That's not even an exaggeration. It stopped for just a second to crawl up into the back of my throat, I think trying to get as far away from the trouble in my uterus as possible.

My face must have looked just as frightened.

"I take it this wasn't planned?" she asked, gazing at me over her clipboard.

No shit, Lady, I thought, *I just asked you about birth control.*

"No," I said, "My daughter just turned a year old."

The doctor nodded, setting her clipboard down on the desk. "There are places I can refer you to if you'd like. There's plenty of time. You aren't far along yet."

She was talking about abortion. But I wasn't sure I could do that.

"I need to talk to the father," I said, "I can't decide anything until I talk to him."

She smiled and nodded at me. "Good," she said, "I was concerned there might not be one."

As I drove away, those are the words I kept repeating in my head. "There might not be one." What if her concerns were valid? What if I had been wrong about Robert's character? I thought back on the times when we had discussed my situation and he had suggested the possibility of pregnancy. He had been completely emotionless. Not fearful or wistful, either. What did that mean?

I started to head to Marjean's house to get Meredith, but decided I couldn't wait. Instead, I drove to where Robert was working. I needed to tell him and see the look on his face. Regardless of what he said, I could look into his eyes, I thought, and know what the outcome would be.

I was crying by the time I got there. I was so

scared.

He was holding a box of tomatoes when he saw me, and I could see the concern in his eyes as he walked towards me, still carrying them.

"What's the matter?" he asked.

I looked at him, still crying, not sure how to say what needed to be said. Finally, I broke down. "I'm pregnant," I wailed.

His concerned look turned to confusion. Then he spoke. "Honey, why are you crying? You scared the hell out of me. I thought it was bad news. This is good. This is real good." He set the tomatoes down and hugged me, and all my worries washed away.

I felt him kiss the top of my head. "When is your lease up?" he whispered, not wanting his step-dad, who was now standing nearby us, to hear.

"I don't have one," I said, "It's a month by month thing."

"I'm off work tomorrow, we'll hunt a house," he said before kissing my cheek. I pulled my face away to see mascara smudged on his white shirt. "Sorry," I laughed.

He looked down at the smudge. "It's okay," he said, "kept it off your cheeks. I'll come by when I get off work, okay?"

I nodded as I turned to walk out. Behind me, I heard Buddy ask "What was that about?"

Robert answered.

"Nothing, Grandpa."

With a new baby on the way, Robert and I married. We also rented a house. And he bought me a washer and dryer so I wouldn't have to carry my clothes to the Laundromat anymore. Things were starting to come together for my weird little family when I was notified that I needed to come to court in case I needed to testify against Dan. He had failed to follow through on one of the terms of his sentencing for a crime had been charged with and convicted of while we were still married, and while I was not officially subpoenaed to appear in court, I had been given a tip that it would be in my best interest to show. I was nervous.

Things with Dan had started calming down. He hardly spoke to me anymore at all, and when he did he was civil most of the time. I feared that my being there was going to cause a disturbance for us, especially with me now beginning to show my pregnancy. The last thing I needed was more stress.

My mother was sick again- not in the hospital, but we all feared that's where she was headed to. I was pregnant again and newly married for the second time. Meredith still was refusing to walk, and her doctor had called in state workers, convinced Meredith had some sort of neurological problem that I was in denial of. I was worried the doctor was right.

I was scared and sad and alone.

I dropped Meredith off at Rob's mom's house and decided to drive around until time for court. I was driving south on Dakota Avenue when a little boy ran out in front of me. So distracted from worrying about everything that was going on, I almost hit him. I didn't even slow down until he was already out from in front of me. When I finally saw him standing there, I slammed my brakes on and slid on some ice into the curb, denting up my front fender. He ran into his house and I sat there for a minute, talking to God. I told Him that if He WAS real, and I was having my doubts, I needed a sign from him that things would be normal again.

When I was finally able to drive again, I kept driving south and wound up near the Humane Society, where I checked my clock and saw I had nearly another hour to kill before court. I decided to stop and look at their animals to pass the time, since I was obviously too nervous to be driving.

When I walked in, there was a kennel on the front desk, and inside it something was shaking. A new catch. The animal control officer picked the kennel up and sat it on a table in front of her. "I have to look this one over, so watch your head- she might be wild." I nodded and, when the kennel door swung upon, a familiar soul stepped out.

There are thousands of stories about cats disappearing miles away from home and then finding their way back home- but Patches had done one better. This had never BEEN her home. She just wound up where I was living and where I needed to see her that day. If this wasn't the sign I'd asked for, I don't know what classifies as one..

I started crying and telling the lady at the desk the story, but she didn't really believe me, I could tell. She told me, though, that she wasn't going to put Patches into the computer system so I could come by after court and just take her because they were overrun with cats anyway.

Court went fine. I didn't even have to talk. Dan noticed I was pregnant, but all he had to say was "Congratulations."

So I went and got my cat and took her home. Sadly, though, she was already very sick and passed away within a week. Kidney failure, the vet said.

But she was there when I needed her to be, and that's all the proof I'll ever need.

At around my twentieth week of pregnancy, I switched doctors because of a disagreement with my physician.

When I switched doctors, there came about some confusion regarding my due date. My original doctor had told me that my baby, who was a girl and to be named Hallie Marie after my sisters, would be due on May 8th. The doctor I switched to insisted that by his calculations, she wasn't due until about June 1st. Because I was angry with my last doctor, I went along with the new one thinking and hoping he was more competent than the last. This was one of many disagreements I had with the doctor. Another was the fact that I was certain Hallie was going to be a boy even though they told me she was a girl after the ultrasounds. I was so sure, in fact, that when Rob and I went to purchase her car seat, I insisted we get a blue one.

At around thirty weeks (by the second doctor's calculations) I started seeing white spots of light, even when standing in total darkness. They looked like fairies. My fingers and ankles began to swell and I started having severe back pains and pre-term contractions.

The house that Robert, Meredith and I were living in had steep steps down to the basement where the washer and dryer were located. Robert was working two jobs at that time and I was home alone with Meredith one night when Meredith threw up on her blankets. I changed her bedding and was carrying the dirty bedclothes downstairs when, halfway down, I became dizzy. The fairies returned, and I couldn't walk any further down the stairs. I sat on the steps for a while to keep from falling and managed to crawl back up into the kitchen and get the telephone. I called Robert to come home and take me to the hospital. I knew something was seriously wrong. I remember sitting on the kitchen floor crying and hoping I wouldn't pass out before he got there because Meredith was still up running around. She was eighteen months old, and had just learned to walk-delayed only by laziness, as her final diagnosis revealed.

Robert made it home within a matter of minutes. It's amazing how fast some men will drive when their wives or children are in danger. He carried Meredith to the car and then came back and carried me. We stopped along the way to leave Meredith with his cousin and he took me to the emergency room.

My blood pressure usually runs about 120/70. When they checked it at the hospital that night, it was 140/90. I was also having contractions about 5 minutes apart. They took me to the maternity ward where the nurses warned us to get ready, with my contractions so regular and my blood pressure so high, they would not be surprised if we had a baby before midnight. When the doctor got there, he told me to stay off my feet, gave me terbuteline to stop the contractions, and sent me home. My blood pressure stayed high for the next 4 weeks and I went into pre-term labor 3 more times. Each time, I was given terbuteline and sent home again, told it was too early to have the baby.

On May 23rd, I was finally able to meet the doctor at the hospital for an induction. My mother, finally back to her old self, made the trip to Huron and stayed at my house with Meredith. The doctor induced my labor and within an hour of receiving the meds, I started having terrible back labor. I was dilated to 1 centimeter the first time the doctor checked me. Hours later, he checked me again and I was still at 1 centimeter. He gave me a couple more hours, checked again, and I was, yet again, still at 1 centimeter. I was in horrible pain, but my doctor could not give me any pain medicine until I reached 4 centimeters. It became clear to Robert and I that this would be a long night.

For twenty-four more hours, I tried to push past 1 centimeter. At six o'clock in the afternoon on the

24th, I was hurting so badly I couldn't take any more. Robert was furious, pacing back and forth in our hospital room when the doctor came in.

"Let's check you again, Jennifer." As he checked, he started chuckling, "this is the damnedest thing I've ever seen, you're STILL only 1 centimeter."

I started crying. I was miserable.

Robert was homicidal. "Isn't there anything else you can do? This has been going on for 24 hours now, she can't do it much longer. She needs something for pain or you need to figure something else out. This shit isn't working."

The doctor and Robert were arguing and I was watching Hallie's heartbeat on the fetal monitor. It began getting slower.

"Doctor.." I called. He didn't hear me and kept arguing with Rob.

"Doctor.." I tried again. He still wasn't paying any attention, so I tried a different approach.

"Rob.." Robert wasn't paying attention either.

Finally, I knew I had to get loud. "THE BABY'S HEART RATE IS DROPPING!"

They both stopped and looked that time. Without hesitation, the doctor started pushing around on my stomach. "Sometimes, the baby moves and the monitor loses the heartbeat, don't panic," he explained.

He continued to move around the monitor before finally paging a nurse. When the nurse came into the room, he told her to do my vitals and then take me down to the operating room. I was going to need a c-section. The nurse did as he asked, which is how she discovered that blood pressure was very high and I had a fever.

She got me ready and they took me down to the operating room where they had to do my vitals again. In the couple of minutes it took to move me from one place to another, my blood pressure had dropped some, but my fever was still quite high. The anesthesiologist came in to give me my epidural and I remember I started shivering. They told me it was a combination of the coldness of the operating room and my fever that was causing me to shake and that made sense to me.

When they finished with the epidural, they laid me down on the table and began prepping for surgery. One of the nurses checked my blood pressure again and it had dropped some more. Because it had dropped twice in a very short amount of time, they sent Robert out of the room. Knowing what I knew from Mom's various hospitalizations, I figured they were afraid something was shutting down, although I never fully understood what the problem was and I was so frantic that I couldn't pay much attention.

I was waiting for my legs to go numb from the epidural and they never did. I could feel them passing things back and forth prepping for surgery and I could feel the paper sheet over me. I looked at the doctor and said "It's not working, I can still feel everything."

He told me I would feel pressure, but no pain.

I said "No, I'm feeling more than pressure." The doctor was assuming I was a scared and nervous patient and merely brushed me off. It was a smart-thinking nurse that rubbed an ice cube across the bottom of my foot. When I jerked my foot back, it was proof that I could still feel more than pressure.

The anesthesiologist started getting ready to try another epidural while the nurse checked my temperature. I had a fever of 103 degrees.

The doctor said "Knock her out, we don't have time to try another epidural."

He then picked up a phone and called a code and at least four more nurses came into the room to assist. They were running and buzzing around so fast, that I became even more disoriented. To this day, I'm not sure what happened to get everyone so frazzled. I know they all looked horrified, though, and I remember thinking to myself that the baby and I probably weren't going to make it. I was in such pain and so tired and so sick and I had seen the baby's heart rate drop.

I thought about Robert in the hall and felt sorry for him and then I thought about Meredith. I fell asleep wondering what would happen to her.

When I woke up in the recovery room, though, Robert was in there with me.

He was crying. My first thought was that we had lost the baby. It didn't dawn on me right away that he was crying because he was scared and upset about what had happened to me.

"Where is he?" I asked him. He laughed at my refusal to believe we had another girl.

"SHE is upstairs in the nursery. They're giving her a little oxygen, but she's okay."

As silly as it is, after everything else, I remember being disappointed to hear she was a girl. I asked him if he ever got to come back in the operating room and he told me that he hadn't, but that the doctor had told him my placenta had already started detaching from the uterus and had started turning brown. The doctor had explained to him that the placenta begins dying at about 42 weeks gestation, so he estimated I was about 2 or 3 weeks overdue. Which means that when I went into labor that night on the basement stairs, she probably should have been born. This also explained why my contractions were not working to help me dilate any faster. They told us that they had to cut my uterus pretty wide to get her out because she and the placenta had become tangled and she was a pretty big baby at nine pounds and six ounces.

The doctor also told us that he would not recommend that we ever try to have another child. After that ordeal, I was fine with this decision.

It was several hours before I was able to hold Hallie because she had to have the oxygen and they wanted my drugs from surgery to wear off.

When they finally brought her to me, I remember thinking she was the most precious thing in the world and I knew right then and there and without hesitation that I would do it all over again a million more times if she needed me to.

The nurse laid her in my arms and she opened her eyes and looked up at me. I was stunned.

The nurse was smiling at us. She put a hand on my shoulder and said, "Go ahead and say something to her. She's waiting to hear your voice so she knows it's you."

Maybe it was the drugs. Or sheer exhaustion. Or maybe I'm an idiot. But I said the only thing I could think of.

"I'm sorry I bought you a blue car seat."

"Most of us become parents long before we have stopped being children."

–Mignon McLaughlin

It was only a couple weeks after Hallie was born that we moved to Tennessee.

When I was sent home from the hospital, I was told to stay off my feet for three weeks, but I couldn't do that. I had packing to do. Hallie came home on May 28th. Robert and I were leaving for Tennessee- permanently- on June eighteenth. My parents were heading south, and I couldn't bare the thought of being without them. Robert, not wanting me to be alone, agreed to move south as well.

Packing was difficult due to the pregnancy and Robert getting in all the hours he could at both his jobs on the last couple weeks in South Dakota before the move. Then, on top of it all, I had a newborn and a toddler to worry about as well as the added stress of leaving behind Marjean and my in-laws and all the people I loved.

My mother marveled at my ability to get up and pack the kitchen the day after returning home from a Cesarean birth, but I thought nothing of it. I had enough of her in me, I guess, that it didn't phase me. She had taught us all well. Every one of us. Hallie gimped around Europe for a full year on her bad ankles when anyone else would have given up and come home. If there was one thing Mama ever taught us it was that it takes a lot more than cancer or bad ankles or a split uterus to keep one of us down.

My days for those few weeks were spent packing and caring for the girls. My mother had to leave after three days to go pack her own house. I had never been so scared as I was watching her drive away knowing I was on my own with them. I turned to see the Hallie in her bouncer, eyes barely opened, looking in my general direction. With one eye anyway. The other was rolling around all over the place, trying to focus in on something colorful, as all baby eyes do.

Meredith sat on the floor next to the bouncer, looking at the baby then me and back at the baby again. This whole ordeal had been very confusing to her. She couldn't understand for the life of her why Robert and I had picked such an ugly pet and why it couldn't just sleep at night instead of scream and cry.

"Do you like your new baby sister?" I asked Meredith, suddenly aware of how much I'd been ignoring her since Hallie was born.

Meredith stared at the baby in deep thought. "Baby loud," she finally explained.

"You were loud when you were a baby, too," I said, "But now it's all better. She'll be your best friend one of these days. You're so lucky to have a sister!" I was trying to get her excited. It wasn't working.

"Okay," she said. That's what she always said when she really didn't understand what someone was explaining to her. It worked.

Hallie was Robert's baby from the beginning. She would cry all day when left with me and Meredith, but the minute he came in from work and picked her up, I wouldn't hear a sound out of her for hours. They'd sit together in the rocker at night and that's where they'd both sleep. When he'd have to put her down to go to work, she would cry for nearly an hour. Even as a newborn, she knew who her daddy was and where he belonged, which was somewhere rocking her.

When she'd scream for him, Meredith would look down into the bassinette at her in disgust. "He comes back," she'd try to explain, knowing it was useless.

Then, she'd give me that look to let me know just what a stupid idea it was bringing that thing home and I should quit putting dresses on it because it looked ridiculous.

When the time came, Robert and I made the entire trip by car with the 2 girls.

I usually like road trips. This was one of the worst I've ever been on.

Hallie hated car rides from the beginning. We

endured hours on end of her screaming to stop, then when we would stop Meredith would scream for us to keep going. What one hated, the other loved.

To make matters worse, we had difficulty finding a hotel room to rest for the night. There was some sort of sports tournament in the first town we stopped and there wasn't a hotel room available within city limits. Then we got lost on our way to the next town, where the only place we could find that had rooms available was, I believe, a renovated mental hospital.

We had to be buzzed into the front door and hallway to our room. The entire place smelled like formaldehyde and curry and all hospital staff was eerily complacent. Robert and I were fumbling with our room key when we saw a member of the Laundry staff drop an entire stack of towels in the hallway and just keep walking, without even looking back, as if someone had sent a radio signal to her brain that she was needed at the front desk and to abort all missions.

Inside the room, the curry smell was even stronger and the lights all flickered in unison. Overhead lights, lamps, even the red power light on the television. Our room either had faulty wiring or a poltergeist. Considering we were locked into the building, we hoped for haunted above ignitable.

We couldn't even shower the next morning. When I turned on the water, all we got was a thick stream of green sludge. We checked out without ever laying eyes on the continental breakfast. We didn't even want to know.

When we got to Tennessee, Robert went to work and, after much talk, the two of us decided that I would remain a stay-at-home mom until the girls were both school age. We rented a two bedroom apartment until we could get on our feet. I hated that apartment.

It was here, though, that I got to experience truly being a Mommy for the first time. We managed to make the apartment work for as long as we needed it to. I got to be home with my babies and it was wonderful.

I hadn't realized how much I loved being a Mommy until then because I was always having to balance being a Mommy and about ten other things all at once. I re-discovered the joy of bunny foo foo and skinnamarink and the itsy bitsy spider.

When Halloween rolled around, I wasn't too tired to go trick-or-treating.

I even loved changing Hallie's diapers. I LOVED it. I got over it, though.

Soon, she was sitting up on her own. Then she said "Mama" and I nearly fainted. I spent my days taking pictures of the girls in various funny poses and lights. I never wanted to forget them being so tiny. I folded all their tiny little clothes and, when Hallie grew out of her newborn sleepers, I bawled. Then I put one on a baby doll and hid the doll in my closet so I could hold it whenever I wanted and re-member her being little. Sick in a way..

Hallie was a super serious baby, though. My sister Hallie used to call Baby Hallie Roberta because she so closely resembled her father. They both have the same worried, serious look all the time.

Baby Hallie didn't laugh at things other kids laughed at. A cartoon character on television would fall off a cliff and Meredith would be rolling with laughter, but Hallie, who we call Sissy, would walk up, look worried, and kiss the screen. She would even look at Meredith sometimes like "How can you be so heartless? Can't you see he just exploded?"

Sissy loved to give baby hugs, too. For as small as she was, she could hug tight.

But Sissy wasn't the only exciting thing happening for Robert and I. We soon bought a house, and then in June of 2006 came something even more exciting.

It was a Friday. Robert and I were sitting on a polished wooden bench outside the courtroom waiting for our turn to see the judge. Two-year-old Meredith was skipping on the marble tile in front of us when she looked up long enough to ask "Daddy, can I go home?"

Daddy, I repeated to myself in thought. This was a word Meredith had probably used thousands of times before, but today it sounded new.

Robert looked up at her and said "Soon, sweetie, we have to talk to somebody important and then we'll go home." Already growing tired and increasingly impatient, Meredith crawled up into his lap and rested her head on his shoulder. He was tired, too. He had worked especially hard this morning at the plant so he could leave in time to be at the courthouse. It was a big day. He was adopting his baby girl.

Dan had given up whatever small amount of interest he had in her long ago. The word "Daddy" held no physical attachments to Meredith. It was, actually, a title that had been earned by the man she was now falling asleep on in the corridor outside Family Court.

I watched them for a while, thinking about how truly blessed we all were for that day. The light was shining off Meredith's blonde curls as they were falling out of her pig tails and spilling over Robert's shoulder and onto his back. She had her thumb in her mouth and her huge, almost sapphire eyes were beginning to close as sleepiness overtook her.

She had her thumb in her mouth.

She never sucked her thumb for anyone but him. He was bouncing his knee- a trick he had used several times before to calm her when she had begun to grow impatient with the grown-up world. This was something he had most commonly done in waiting rooms before doctor and physical therapy appointments that he had accompanied me to for her since she was six months old.

Our lawyer appeared and waved us into the courtroom. Robert walked in first, still carrying Meredith on his shoulder and I followed behind him. We were instructed to take a seat at a table facing the judge. Robert sat Meredith in her chair, but she got up and started trying out several other chairs. I turned to correct her, but the bailiff shook his head and said to let her be.

The interview with the judge is blurred in my memory. I know we were there for quite a while, but I don't remember much of what was said. The judge had asked Robert if he was fully aware of the responsibility he was taking on and if he acknowledged that, in the event of our divorce, he would be held liable for child support. Robert said "I've always taken care of her as my own and have always intended to do my best to take care of her forever."

As he was saying this I was watching his face. He was calm and collected, as usual. I began noticing his shoulders. They seemed broad to me, slightly slumped in his fatigue from an especially hard morning at work, but they still looked strong. They looked like my own daddy's shoulders.

Meredith was singing to herself somewhere in the row of seats behind us. The bailiff was chuckling. She must have patted the seat next to her because I heard the sound of a little hand slapping upholstery and the slurred "wanna sit?" that come's from being two years old, tired, and overly friendly.

"I can't," the bailiff had chuckled back in a quiet voice, almost whispering. The judge looked up, smiling. I looked around and saw that everyone in the room was smiling with him. "They're nothing but love at that age," I heard someone say.

The judge pointed at Robert. "Meredith?" he asked, "who is this man?"

"That's my daddy," she said.

The next thing I remember, Robert had Meredith

on his shoulders and we were walking to the car.

I clutched the adoption papers the entire way home. I clutched them so hard, in fact, that twice I stopped and looked at them for fear the heat of my hand might cause the ink to smear, making it illegible that she was, in fact, his now.

That we were all officially a family.

*"Promise me you'll never forget me, because if I
thought you would I'd never leave."*

–Winnie the Pooh

Our first year in Tennessee was a happy one. Mama was well. She and Daddy thrived as grandparents, not only to my children but to Laura's as well. Mama loved being a grandma.

Every Sunday, Mama would cook a big meal and the whole family would come to her house and be together, which we hadn't been able to do in years. She was particularly fond of Meredith, who had turned into a fun-sized version of herself.

Meredith was mischievous. She liked to prowl through her Grandmother's things and try to sneak outside when nobody was looking. She would gaze out the back door at Mama's house at Mama's little brown car with glossed over eyes and a furrowed brow. She was thinking if she could just get out the door and into that driver's seat, she could go anywhere.

Mama called Meredith "Tootie" and they both referred to that little brown car as "Tootie's car."

When Mama was cooking or doing dishes, she would set Meredith up on the counter top in the kitchen, so Meredith could sneak sugar from the sugar bowl. They both thought I was too stupid to know that's what they were doing. Sometimes, I would complain about it to Mama and tell her she was ruining Meredith's teeth, but it never did any good. I gave up after a while and just put extra emphasis on the importance of oral hygiene.

Mama loved Sissy, too. Especially when she just wanted a sleeping buddy. They would lay on Mama's bed and sleep the afternoon away. Sissy would always have a handful of Mama's now completely gray hair. When Mama and I would get a chance to sit down together and talk, she would always reach for my hand, and give it that hand squeeze of hers. If I were to go blind, I would always know my Mama by the way she squeezed my hand.

Me and Mama talked about anything and everything we could think of. When I wasn't at her house, we spent most of our day on the phone.

But Mama started getting sick again. Slowly, at first, then she started having bleeding when she would use the bathroom and decided to see a doctor, who told her she had scarring in her large intestine, probably from the infection she suffered after her gastric bypass. She would need surgery to remove her colon and, as was the plan, create a new colon from a piece of her large intestine. They called this procedure a J-Pouch. Mama said it sounded like something you could buy at Toys R Us.

Mama was, understandably, scared to have another surgery. But she was told she wouldn't survive another ten years without it and she desperately wanted to see her grandchildren grow up.

She had the surgery on my daddy's birthday. November tenth. Soon after, she was able to come home and spend her first night in the house she and Daddy had just bought, but returned to the hospital the next day, having gotten sick again. MRSA was back and the J-Pouch was not healing correctly due to Mama's diabetes. She was in trouble.

They put Mama in ICU. Daddy made the trip to Memphis to be with her, and stayed there for days on end, only coming home when he needed to shower and change clothes. Carrie was living with Hallie at the time in town, sharing a house with another friend. With Mama sick, the two of them moved home to help Daddy.

I had my girls and wasn't able to do as much for Daddy or Mama as I wanted to. I couldn't even go see Mama as often as I would have liked because the girls weren't allowed into the ICU wing at the hospital and Robert was working long hours, unable to stay home with them every time I wanted him to. I would go see Mama on weekends when I would get the chance, but I've never been good with stuff like that. She just laid there, mostly, confused and unable to talk from multiple tubes running in and out of her body. I hated to see her like that, and she hated being seen.

So I would never stay long. Just long enough for her to ask how the girls were and if I was okay. I might tell her something silly I saw on television about one of her favorite celebrities and she'd laugh a little, usually, but sometimes that only confused her. Because of her pain medication and the fever from her infection, she became confused easily.

Once, I was talking to her about Denzel Washington and she cut me off to say, "You know he's a really nice guy. And he likes pudding. Remember that time he came to see us and he ate all that pudding?"

We had been told not to play along, but correcting her only made her upset. So we played along anyway. It was the least cruel of our options. "No, Mama," I said, "What kind of pudding was it?"

When Mama couldn't remember what she was talking about, or if she thought she might be confused, her answer was always the same. "Oh, you know.."

Mama stayed in that hospital for months, but as she drew closer to her one hundred and twentieth day, when her insurance was to run out, the hospital became increasingly impatient with the situation. Eventually, a Social Worker waited and watched for any family to come visit so she could pounce at them with questions about where we planned to take Mama. They didn't want her if we couldn't pay, regardless of how sick she still was.

Mama's situation was the same, if not worse, as it had been the day she was admitted. They eventually had to remove the J-pouch entirely and insert a colostomy, but the original colostomy did not heal and had to be redone, leaving a hole in her stomach that food dribbled out of whenever she tried to eat. Soon, that hole filled up with infection.

Even her I.V.s were falling out. Her body was so busy trying to fight away her infection that it wasn't able to heal itself. It became clear to us all that if the infection didn't kill her, she'd starve. This was Mama's last time.

Towards the end of Mama's hospital stay, Carrie and I called the hospital to get permission to bring the girls to see Mama. Mama had been asking to see my daughters, probably afraid she never would again. The nurse we spoke to told us it would be fine as long as the girls did not sit on the bed.

So Carrie and I dressed the girls and loaded them into my car and took off for Memphis. When we arrived, we stopped in the gift shop so Meredith could take her beloved grandma a present. She picked out two ceramic angels. One had blue eyes and blond hair like her, the other brown eyes and red hair like Sissy. She clutched them in her little hands all the way up the elevator, so pleased at the gift she had picked out for Mama.

We got to Mama's floor and walked into the hospital room. Meredith's excitement turned suddenly into confusion and fear.

Mama's I.V. pole was beeping with an empty bag hanging from it. Carrie and I could smell urine as we walked into the room. And Mama was crying.

"It's been beeping for an hour," Mama weakly explained, "And I peed myself waiting on a bed pan."

Carrie and I were furious. I opened the door and looked towards the nurses station where a middle-aged redhead sat laughing on her cell phone. I waved my hand until she saw me standing there, then motioned for her to come to me. When she did, Carrie, who was standing behind me, snarled, "Why is our mother laying in here like this with the door shut?"

The nurse looked embarrassed. Like she'd been caught with her hand in a cookie jar. As she walked into the room, trying to think up an excuse, she saw my girls sitting on the small sofa seat near the window. "Those kids can't be in here," she snapped, happy to have something to shift the blame on.

"We called ahead and were given permission to bring them," I said, "And that doesn't have anything to do with the fact that my mother's been sitting here for an hour listening to her I.V. pole beep. She needs fluids constantly, not just whenever you get done gossiping to whoever."

Before I could finish my lamenting, Carrie noticed something I hadn't. She motioned towards Mama's bedside table and asked, "Why is her phone off the hook? Were you afraid she'd call someone?"

Flabbergasted, the nurse tried to explain, "If we'd had any idea you were bringing your kids up today, arrangements could have been made."

This angered me more. "Arrangements? What

arrangements? You would have cleaned her up a little? I didn't realize we had to make an appointment to see our own mother, but seeing how you treat her I can certainly understand the necessity."

This made the nurse angry. She wanted me gone, and used the only way she could think of to try and make me leave.

"The kids can't be here," she snarled, "You have to go."

"I'm not going anywhere," I said. Carrie stood next to me, relaying the message she wasn't leaving, either.

About that time, the phone which Carrie had reconnected only moments prior rang.

"I bet that's my dad," I smiled, "Excuse me."

Carrie beat me to the phone, though, and answered. I was right. Carrie turned, looking at the nurse and smiled. "Daddy, there's a problem here. This nurse is telling us we have to take the kids and leave and we just got here and we called ahead and got permission this morning."

There was a pause while Daddy talked.

"No," Carrie continued, "Everyone saw us walk in with the girls. It only became a problem when we asked the nurse why Mom's I.V. bag was empty and beeping and why she was laying in her own pee in here with the door shut."

About that time, the red headed nurse completely lost her cool. She started screeching excuses, one after another. She sounded ridiculous. Childish. She was so loud, I couldn't hear Carrie anymore. Daddy couldn't, either. Carrie stopped talking abruptly and handed the phone to the nurse. "He wants to talk to you," she said.

The nurse got on the phone and began explaining her side of the story, which consisted mostly of a list of excuses about my mother being difficult to work with and Carrie and I being rude. I heard Daddy's voice, but his words were indecipherable. I could tell by his tone that he was angry. The nurse's face flashed red, almost matching her hair. "Fine," she hissed through tight lips, "I'll go get her."

Mama laid in the bed crying as we waited for the nurse to return with her supervisor. "I'm sorry," Mama said.

"Don't be sorry," Carrie replied, "It's not your fault."

Mama turned to look at the girls, still in the sofa seat, to smile and wave. The girls, equally confused, waved back, but sat silent and watched.

When the supervisor and nurse returned to the room, the supervisor got on the phone to talk to Daddy. The nurse stood, arms folded in front of her, smugly smiling at Carrie and I. She now looked like a little kid that had just snitched out a classmate to the teacher. I rolled my eyes at her. She glared at me.

"Normally we try to be respectful of people," Carrie explained, "Particularly old ladies. But nobody treats Mama this way."

Around that time, the supervisor hung up the phone. "They had permission to bring the kids up here," she explained to the nurse.

"Nobody told me," the overgrown child whined, "And they started in on me about her I.V. bag being empty and all kinds of stuff. I've been busy."

"She was sitting at the nurses station talking on her cell phone," I interjected, "And Mama's bag is still empty. The pole is still beeping. And in case you can't smell, she's laying in her own pee."

The supervisor looked around the room, then back at the nurse.

"Go home," she said, "Just go home. I've got this."

The redheaded nurse left the room crying. Normally I would feel bad. I'm pretty sure we had just gotten her fired. But I was happy. Victorious. I didn't know how the other nurses would treat Mama when we couldn't be there, but at least Carrie and I had eliminated a bad one.

I hated leaving her there that day. I stayed until she was cleaned up and her I.V. was dripping fluids again and we could talk, but Mama was tired and wanted us to go. I could tell.

Driving home that night, Meredith kept pointing at the moon. She was as amazed by it as I had been all those years ago when I had asked Alice why it followed me. I looked up at it and thought of Alice and Grandma Hallie and now Mama and realized that all the grown ups had gotten old and were dying. Even Aunt Camille, as beautiful as I always believed her to be, now had gray hair. My Daddy's hair was nearly all white.

Even I had a few grays. But I didn't feel any

different than I had when I was six. My thoughts were, basically, the same. Only now I was bigger and could drive a car. And, somehow, there were two more little people in the world depending on me now. I wondered if Mama felt the same.

On the one hundred and twenty-first day of Mama's hospital stay- the day her insurance ran out- the social worker was waiting for Daddy when he arrived at Mama's room.

"She has to go somewhere," she had stated, explaining that the hospital could now do nothing for her.

She offered to set him up with hospice caregivers and an ambulance ride home for Mama, where Daddy was instructed to just let her die.

With no money or insurance to pay for a second opinion, and no way of talking the hospital into keeping her, Daddy had to make arrangements for Mama's homecoming.

Hallie, Carrie, Laura, and I helped him clean the house and prepare for Mama to return. He fixed a place in their oversized bedroom with a hospital bed near the window so Mama could look outside. Next to the bed, he pulled up a rocking chair so he could sit with her throughout the day and he mounted a television set nearby so she could watch her favorite shows. It wasn't ideal, but it was all he could do for her.

When he made the trip back to Memphis to sign her out of the hospital, Hallie and I waited at home for the hospice caseworker. The caseworker arrived shortly after Mama and Daddy did. The two men driving the ambulance helped Daddy get Mama into the bed and comfortable and showed him how to use Mama's oxygen machine, which was bulky and loud as it rattled against the hardwood floors. Daddy put a blanket underneath it, which muffled the sound a little, but it was still too loud. Mama had grown used to strange sounds, though, in her weeks at the hospital and hardly noticed.

The caregiver instructed us to give Mama whatever she wanted. What was important now was not healing her, but keeping her comfortable. Mama was confused in the house, having only ever spent one night there before. She thought she had been taken to a new hospital. A worse one.

Although Mama was now close by, I found it hard to spend as much time with her as I wanted. I never knew what to say to her, and I felt like if I didn't talk to her, I was being rude. Sometimes I'd take the kids to her house, hoping they'd bring about conversation, but Sissy was only interested in Mama's oxygen mask and Meredith was afraid. She would stand out on the front porch and put her nose against the glass of the window, looking in at Mama from a safe distance. We all told her that was Grandma, but we could tell that she didn't quite believe it. Her grandma didn't look like that. Her grandma was prettier. And more energetic.

As time wore on, Mama's pain and confusion got worse. She would get angry at her nurses, and sometimes at us, for no reason.

One night, I was sitting with Mama and she looked at me, tearfully, and mouthed "I'm dying."

I knew she was. But I thought I should comfort her, so I said, "No you aren't, Mama. You're just sick." She looked at me, saddened. I don't know if she was sad that I would lie, or sad because she didn't know I knew better. But I felt guilty. Like she needed to talk about dying, and I'd cheated her out of the opportunity.

Hallie and Daddy provided most of her care at the end. Hallie should not have had to carry that cross for all three sisters, but she was better at it than I was. I never knew what to do for Mama. I was always afraid I'd say something that would upset her more, or I wouldn't say enough and that would make her sad, too. Hallie knew what Mama wanted and needed better than I did in those last days, and she was an angel to our mother.

Carrie, being the baby, was also upset by Mama's situation and often made plans to provide herself an excuse to be away from home, where she didn't have to think about it so much.

I think Daddy held out hope right until the end that Mama would get up out of bed and be fine. Miraculously. Just as she had all the other times.

In a way, I think we all expected that.

I was shopping when she died. I was supposed to be on my way to her house because the doctor had been there that morning and told Daddy she was on her way out. But when Daddy had called to tell me, I guess I felt like we'd heard that so many times before that I didn't believe it.

I was on my way to her house and thought that, just in case, I should buy a black skirt. I stopped at the mall. It seems silly now. But I bought my skirt, knowing there was a funeral coming soon. When I made it to Daddy's, she was already gone.

You hear people refer to "deafening silence" and you think it's some dramatic overstatement until you really DO hear it. I opened the front door to deafening silence. Her oxygen machine was not running. I knew exactly what that meant. My heart twisted in my chest because I knew before I ever walked into the bedroom what I would find. She was just laying there. My daddy sat beside her, waiting for someone to come take her away.

I stayed with Daddy for a few minutes, until he told me I needed to go to Laura's, where my other sisters were waiting for me.

I got into my car and was driving to Laura's house, down a gravel road that reminded me much of the road we lived on in Yale. I was thinking about Mama, and her life. And what a remarkable person she was and how my girls probably would never remember her, despite how much she adored them.

It was a sunny day out. Birds were chirping and flying through the sky and across the road in front of me. Mother cows were cleaning their calves at the side of the road and wildflowers were growing around fence posts. Even magnolias were blossoming from the trees in peoples yards as I drove by.

But inside my car, it was raining. And I was cold, and alone. My heart was broken and I was finding it hard to breathe. I felt scared.

I felt like an orphan.

"A funeral is for those left behind. Sometimes, one wonders if the weeping is more out of fear for ourselves than it is sympathy for the deceased."

–Deng Ming-Dao

Daddy planned Mama's funeral alone. She had mentioned before that she wanted to be buried pretty in pink, and Daddy kept that in mind when he visited the funeral home.

He wouldn't let anybody go with him. I think he was afraid we'd try to talk him out of his choices. But we wouldn't have. He did a beautiful job.

We buried her on Mother's Day weekend alongside her mother in the Edgewood Cemetery. The very spot she had stood years before and told us her stories of Ruskin Cave and the summers she spent on Yellow Creek with her cousins would now be where she spent eternity. At least she'd been happy there.

The very cousins she spoke of were now her pallbearers.

The funeral was at the Edgewood Church, but the viewing was in Dickson at the Dickson Funeral home. The same place both Mama's parents had been taken when they died.

Daddy chose the Rose room for Mama. Her casket was ivory with little pink roses painted on the top and pink lining. Mama's sisters dressed her in a black suit with a pink blouse underneath. She looked young again. Pretty and healthy. She looked like Mama.

At the funeral home, the second wave sat together and watched as all the important people in Mama's life funneled in to bid her farewell. People we'd never met, but heard about, came in suddenly adding faces to the stories we'd grown up hearing.

The people we did know all wanted to hug us, which I wasn't entirely comfortable with, but I allowed it as to not appear rude. Some people asked where Robert and the girls were.

I had told Robert not to come. Funerals, in my opinion, are no place for kids and they would be afraid if left home with anyone other than one of their parents. Instead, I carried a picture of them in my purse to show people who were interested. Nearly all of them commented on how similar Meredith and my mother looked, which opened the door for me to tell them how much Meredith and Mama loved one another. It was a relief, in a way, because it provided me with something to discuss. I hate making small talk. It's never been easy for me.

Helen drove down from Michigan for the funeral. She and Gail had parted ways years prior and Helen was now working in Michigan at a college. She drove straight through, and was exhausted when she arrived. But she wouldn't have missed the funeral.

Without Robert there, I tried to keep Helen company, knowing she was also there alone.

Even Frank's sons-Wesley and Zachary- were able to come. Zachary had been four when we saw him last. Wesley was only twelve. When Sandy, their mother and Frank's ex wife, heard the news of Mama's passing, she brought the boys to Tennessee for the funeral. They had grown.

Wesley now stood taller than Daddy and Zachary looked like Frank. They had both gotten so smart and polite. It was obvious that Sandy had done well with them. She raised gentlemen.

When we made our way to Edgewood Church, I sat beside Daddy in the front row. Hallie sat to my right, and Carrie to her right. And on the other side of Carrie was Laura and her family.

Wesley and Zachary sat behind me and Daddy.

The Edgewood church pastor, a nice older lady that sang parts of her sermon, gave a beautiful speech about Mama and death, and we were able to play the two songs Mama had always wanted us to play for her.

Far Side Banks of Jordan was played for Daddy, who couldn't make it through without crying. Zachary reached an arm forward and rested a hand on Daddy's shoulder as he cried. Wise beyond twelve, he understood that was all anyone could do.

Next, we played *Ripple*. There was controversy over that one. But, in the end, it worked well. Everyone loved it. A few of the pallbearers even sang along. But I didn't understand at the time why Mama had wanted it played.

That would come weeks later.

I had the song on a CD in my car that I had been listening to since the funeral. It was on a CD I had made for myself full of songs that reminded me of Mama. Mostly Rolling Stones with some Nancy Griffith, John Prine, and the funeral songs thrown in.

I was on my way home from church when I figured out why she had asked us to play it.

There's a line in the song that goes "There's a road, no simple highway." I had always heard those lyrics and interpreted them "There's a road, no.. a simple highway." That's not what they are. They're saying "There's a road" but it is "no simple highway." Once I figured out that part, the rest of it came to me.

The song begins with questions:

If my words did glow with the gold of sunshine
And my tunes were played on the harp unstrung,
Would you hear my voice come through the music?
Would you hold it near, as it were your own?

Right after asking these things, it gets a little more complicated, lapsing into apology. The type we all run into in life, when we're trying to say something but we know the words aren't there. "Sorry if I don't say this right, but here's what I'm thinking, anyway, because it needs to be said.."

It's a hand me down, the thoughts are broken.
Perhaps, they're better left unsung.
I don't know. Don't really care.
Let there be songs to fill the air.

Using this song, Mama was getting through her last message to us. I just hadn't pieced it together yet.

When you take out the metaphors in the song, it makes perfect sense. It was just a matter of breaking the metaphors.

The song, much like Mama's life, doesn't try to stick to one theme. Neither does grief.

What Mama was trying to say was "You have to do this yourself. Nobody can grieve for you, but you are all grieving. While you're alone, you really aren't. You have each other."

Then the song made sure we understood the following verse:

...And if you go, no one may follow
That path is for your steps alone...

Just because the others don't grieve the way we do, doesn't mean they aren't grieving.

Mama knew some of us, mostly me, were awkward. She knew emotions aren't an easy thing for us to convey all the time. But she wanted us to know she understood that no matter how we grieved, we were grieving. And she wanted us to understand each other, too. She couldn't leave this world without bossing us one last time.

I could almost hear her. "Be good to your sisters."

When Mama died, it turned our worlds completely upside down. Everything seemed empty. And I think we all felt alone.

But yet, we weren't alone. We all lost our mother. Daddy lost his wife. Aunts and Uncles lost a sister. We were all grieving her. The same person. Stretched out across the country were people missing Mama. She had never been on television. Never wrote a symphony or ran for office. But people everywhere mourned her.

And while the knowledge that I was not the only one missing my mother didn't thwart my loneliness, it found room to live beside it. And I found comfort there.

The song ends with *La-de-da-da-d*a, everyone singing together in harmony.

And that's what she wanted us to know. We have one another. We all had the common sadness that comes with losing a loved one- be it a mother, a friend, or a whatever.

And she couldn't suffer for us nor could she tell us how to suffer. Her final message was simply to be there for each other to lean on, and not be afraid to lean. We would make it.

Let it be known, there is a fountain..

"I'm in a better place," she was whispering, "Help each other."

And maybe I'm wrong. Maybe my thoughts are broken.

Perhaps, after all, they were better left unsung.

I don't know.

I don't really care.

"You came into my life, turned it upside down, and now it all makes more sense."

–Kat Given

I t's been six months since my mother died, and it gets a little easier every day.

There are times when I wake up, and in the groggy moments between sleep and reality, I wonder how she's doing today. Other times, one of the children will say something funny, or I'll forget the recipe for homemade beef stew and I'll reach for the phone to call her.

But on some days I make it past noon before she crosses my mind.

Carrie's moved to Washington. I guess she figured it was time to set out on her own. She has a good job and is planning to come back to Tennessee to visit soon. It's been awful quiet since she's been gone.

Hallie is still in town, and I see her at least once a week. We get away alone once in a while and rent movies or have dinner and talk about the silliness of our childhood. It's nice to have her nearby. I think she is planning to return to school next year.

Frank is re-married, and works with the railroad. He travels a lot, but always finds time to come see his little sisters when he's in town.

Laura and her family are doing well and as of lately she has been busying herself with remodeling her kitchen.

Daddy stays gone all the time. He says his boss keeps him busy, but I think being on the road is easier than being home. He's used to being by himself in the truck. Being by himself in his own house is new, and probably a little scary. I can't imagine the quiet.

I do think of Mama daily, though, and wonder what she'd think of the changes in our family. Or if the changes would have ever taken place had she been here.

My girls are getting bigger by the minute. I look at Sissy sometimes and think about how Mama would laugh at all her red hair. As Sissy's hair gets longer and redder, her soul gets softer. She's the most caring child I've ever come across in all my life- almost to a fault. I worry she'll get herself hurt. People as kind as her always do, it seems. If the meek will inherit the earth, Hallie will get Asia and all the oceans.

Meredith is Hallie's opposite. She's loud. She soaks up attention. She's, for lack of a better word, devious. My mother would be so proud. Meredith got all the best parts of Dan and myself, and my mother spent the three years they had together polishing them. Meredith has been referred to as "mini Margaret," and I don't think another name would suit her better.

All this time without Mama has left me with a lot of time to think. I used to spend my days on the phone with Mama. Now, I spend them at home, trying to make sense of this life and all we encounter on our way through it, and the more I think the more confused I get. But there are some things I think I'm starting to figure out.

You see, the way I see it is the meaning of a person's life can be something major that will always be remembered by the masses- like the lives of Martin Luther King, Jr., or Albert Einstein, or Mother Theresa.

But it can also be something simple, and seemingly meaningless. Like Mama's, or Grandma's, or Alice's. Or even Patches.

Before you picked up this book, these lives meant nothing to you. They still may not.

As I remembered them, though, and put them on paper, I could see them as vividly as if they were sitting here in front of me. I could hear Mama's voice- sweet and soft. I could smell the coffee grounds and bananas in Grandma's pantry. I heard the ticking of the cat clock in Alice's kitchen.

And Patches laid warm at my feet.

And I know that the meaning of their lives was to be a part of other lives.

I think about my cousins, aunts, uncles, and siblings and realize how many children these ladies loved. And how many children loved them. How many people.

I can't pay any of them back for what they gave me. That is a debt that has to be collected by new children who will hopefully hand it down someday when they find they can't repay me.

And so I wrote this whole crazy story out, word by word sentence by sentence page by page in the hopes that, someday, someone will pick one of the ten copies I'll be lucky to sell up from some bargain bin somewhere and learn what I learned from the ones that fill its pages.

The meaning of life is to help each other through it.

Kindness trickles, and somewhere down the stream I guarantee somebody is going to have their lives touched as a result of whatever little bit of good I do today. Maybe they will do something huge. Maybe not. But that's just how it works.

Cancer, diabetes, and heart failure kill people every day. Old cats get sick. Single mothers struggle. Doctors make mistakes. Children get picked on in school. Everything you own could burn to ash in a few hours. Parents are gone before we know it. The world can be dark.

So we carry sunshine in our pockets and we use it to light our way. When someone's sunshine burns out, we relight it from our own and keep moving forward, together, onto whatever comes next.

And, sometimes, it gets so cold that everyone's sunshine starts to burn out. At times in my life, the flame has disappeared, leaving nothing but a glowing rock. It's happened to everyone, I imagine.

But the magic of hope is that when this happens, daylight is just around the corner. And when you make it through the cold darkness of night, that little rock will burst into flame again, hotter and brighter than ever before.

And each time this happens, the flame will last a little longer.

Until the last time, when it will join the sun in the sky and burn on forever, reigniting the flames of the pieces it leaves behind.

Lightning Source UK Ltd.
Milton Keynes UK
UKHW01f1840140818
327243UK00001B/12/P